I Love You Dad

I Love You Dad

By Russell and **David McCain,** with special
contributions from **Thomas McCain**

In honor of our
Fathers and Families.
GO IRISH!

I Love You Dad

Dedication. To the irrevocable, irretractable, and immeasurable bond of love that is and should exist between all fathers and sons.

Thank you. I thank God for every minute of every day that I get to spend with my family: my wife Margarita and my two sons Johnny and Danny.

Special thanks to Uncle Tom for his contributions to the telling of my Dad's story, but, more importantly, for sharing with me my Dad's pride in our undertaking The Drive, and for encouraging me to continue writing about and loving my Dad.

Photo information.

Front Cover—Father and Son: Russell and David McCain, July 1990, Bristol, CT.

Back Cover—Front row, left to right: David McCain, Thomas McCain, Russell McCain, Alena McAdoo, Colleen McAdoo. Back row left to right: Richard McCain, Marion McAdoo, Andrea McAdoo. Circa 1941, Osgood Avenue, New Britain, CT.

Table of Contents

Introduction.

And so it was, the telling of the extraordinary life of a seemingly ordinary man who was anything but. Never is there a more influential life than that of a father on a son. Automatically a hero, revered and awed. Let me tell you about mine, Russell Francis McCain, in his own words and recollections of everyday life and experiences from the 1930s to the present.

Before we begin in earnest, my Dad—Russell—was born January 15, 1931, in Nashua, New Hampshire. He was 80 when we started writing, strong as an ox, smart as a whip, and as humble as God can make a man, although he had no reason to be. He had his collection of ailments accumulated

1

over the years: heart disease, diabetes, recurring cancer, an aneurism, a failing kidney (one was removed at age 79), lungs ravaged by 50 years of smoking, and many more, although he never complained about or ever mentioned them.

He gently and peacefully passed on April 22, 2012, at 81 years old, and we kept writing, talking and loving each other to the end....

However, back to the origins of this book. I remember telling my Dad at Christmas just before his 80th birthday that we were going to a seminar so that we could write his biography. "Free snacks and juice," I told him. He gave me that accepting smile and those warm eyes that I had seen dozens if not hundreds of times before, shook his head slightly back and forth, tilted his head to the side, and quietly agreed to go with the shrug of his shoulders. I could tell he really didn't want to do anything of the sort but that he likely reconciled himself to going, figuring that we could spend a few quality hours alone together and, of course, for the free snacks and juice.

Introduction.

While I'll never truly know whether he enjoyed the seminar, we did enjoy our time together as we always do, even if little is actually said. On the rainy night drive home, however, something quiet and wonderful happened. My Dad started telling me stories about his life, many of which I had never heard, or at least not heard in such detail, ever before. I could tell at that moment that we were about to embark on a warm and heartfelt journey.

as it took off lickety-split for the barn. The horse made it through the gate but unfortunately Richard and the rake didn't. Richard didn't get hurt (only his feelings), but the harness and the gate had to be repaired.

It was about this time that my aunt Pauline McAdoo died and my Uncle George and his four girls came to live with us for a while. The girls—Marion, Andrea (Topsy), Alena (Lee), and Colleen—were all within a few months of being the same age as us four boys. We all got along well together and thought it was novel and fun. The four McAdoo boys were in the service.

That summer, my father and Uncle George decided to have a good old-fashioned New England clam bake for some of the guys who came to Connecticut with them in the foundry business and for the friendly neighbors who were so generous to us all. They went to Rhode Island and came back loaded with seaweed, clams, corn, lobsters, etc. We dug holes in the ground, built fires in them, added rocks, seaweed, bags with corn, clams, lobsters, and potatoes and covered with more seaweed and canvas. After a few hours and many games of horseshoes, we set up the tables and benches and uncovered the pits. What a feast for friends and neighbors. Later that fall construction started on a "housing project" in the fields adjoining our house and we spent our last Christmas at 469 Osgood Avenue.

Between Christmas and New Year 1944 we moved to 169 Fairview Drive, Kensington, Connecticut. For me, that was grade seven. We moved to a brand new ranch-style house in a newly constructed project. We were about the third family to move into this project of some 150 dwellings. That winter, I started a newspaper route (*New Britain Herald*) in the project. It lasted for years, and I later passed it on to my brother David, and he in turn passed it on to our brother Tommy.

In the early 1940s, because of the war industry, there was a huge influx of people to Connecticut, New Britain in particular, which was known as the "hardware city." This caused a real shortage of housing. The government addressed this by building "housing projects," some more permanent than others. Ours in Kensington was of the permanent type and is still a nice, well-kept area of now privately owned homes. Berlin, of which Kensington is a part, was one of the earliest settled and founded towns in Connecticut. In fact, New Britain, at one time, was an annex of Berlin.

So, Berlin was a classic representation of an old New England town. The old graves with notable and old headstones, historically registered homes, school houses and churches, farm lands, orchards, a water-powered factory, and a major and busy railway station (halfway between New York and Boston). Another major industry was the making of Stiles & Reynolds red building bricks from the natural red clay soil. There were a number of ponds around the area we lived in (some quite large, like several acres or more). They were the holes left from digging the clay, and when they struck water and it came in faster than they could pump it out, they moved their equipment and let them fill up. Eventually they became great ponds for swimming and fishing. Most were quite isolated and off the beaten path, and it was not uncommon to go "skinny dipping" with the guys.

(I remember one such locally famous body of water called "Steam Shovel Pond" that my Dad always pointed out to me whenever we drove by. The story he told was that when the steam shovel operator struck water in this particular clay pit, the water came in so fast they couldn't move the shovel out of the pond fast enough before it became covered with water, all but the very top of the crane boom. He even told me one of his boyhood friends saved the operator's life when his friend pulled the operator out of the steam shovel cab from which the operator had sustained a broken neck while trying to escape. True, false, or somewhere in between I'll never know, but, a story nonetheless that I have enjoyed passing on to both of my sons. Back to my Dad....)

It was always a mystery to me how the fish got started in these ponds. I mean all kinds, not just bull heads and eels, but perch, blue gills, bass, and crappie— plentiful and good size. I've spent many happy hours alone or with my buddies, brothers and father fishing there, and later, even with my wife once or twice.

January 1944, wow, everything is new. The town, house, school—I didn't know anybody and no one knew me. They didn't know I was shy and I'm not telling. My new school was attached to the high school. We were grades kindergarten through seven; the high school, eight through twelve. I was in grade seven, the big shots of the elementary school, plus I was a pretty big and strong guy (different from Washington Junior High in New Britain, which was grades seven through nine, where we were the newbies to be picked on). Being a newcomer brought attention but I made it a point to show that I wasn't a bully nor would I be bullied. By the time summer came I had a lot of everlasting friends.

(Here I must interject and share a story my Dad told me several times. At his prior school he was picked on more often than not. He did not want that to happen again. So, on

the first day of school, he walked up to the biggest ninth grader he could find (my Dad was in seventh), and said, "Nobody's going to pick on me," and punched the ninth grader in the nose. He was sent to the principal's office, his parents were called in, he had a week's detention, but no one ever picked on him again, or so the story goes.)

Chapter 2: Family and the Military

My father, Francis Albert McCain, born November 12, 1902, was the youngest of the three sons of Frances McCain, those sons being Elwell, Henry, and Francis, was too young for World War I but was in the Army. I've seen pictures of him in an Army uniform by a tent, with knickers-type pants, leg wrappings, boots, and a broad-brimmed hat. For some reason, I believe he was in the Coast Artillery. I don't know if Elwell ever served. Henry fought in the Army in Europe in the trenches and collected a pension for various wounds and for being gassed. My father, Francis, was too old for service in World War II. None of the McCain boys (Richard, Russell (me), David, or Thomas) were old enough to serve in World

War II but Richard, David, and I were drafted into the Army. Thomas was in the Army Reserve. Richard went in before the Korean War and spent his time in the U.S. and on Atoll Island, off of Alaska, near Japan. I missed Korea and, after basic training, was sent to Japan. David also went to Japan following basic training. Tom went to his monthly reserve meetings and summer camps but was never activated.

The McAdoo boys—my cousins and the sons of George and Pauline McAdoo (Pauline was my mother's sister), Olin, Paul, Raymond and Edwin—all served in World War II. Olin was drafted into the Army and served most of his time in England and Europe. Paul, in the Navy, was a diesel mechanic on a submarine in the Atlantic. Later, Paul was transferred, by request, to LTS duty (landing troop ship) in the Pacific after learning that his brother Raymond had been killed on Iwo Jima. Raymond had been wounded on a previous landing on a Pacific island; he lost an ear and was eligible to come home, but opted to stay with his battalion (Marines) for their next landing: Iwo Jima. Edwin was also a Navy man, being the youngest; I don't think he saw any action. When the war was over, all of the McAdoo boys except Raymond came home and relocated to Connecticut, got married, and had families.

Chapter 3: My Parents

I really don't know the background of how my parents met, but I assume it all occurred in or around Nashua, New Hampshire, because they both grew up there. I've seen where they went to school—my father through grade eight and my mother through high school.

My mother, Irene Lucier, had two sisters: Pauline, who married George McAdoo, and Hazel, who married but I don't know who to. George and Pauline lived in Hudson, New Hampshire (a small town just outside of Nashua, like Terryville to Bristol). They had eight children—four boys (Olin, Paul, Raymond, and Edwin) and four girls (Marion, Andrea (Topsy), Alena and Colleen). Hazel lived in Pepperell, Massachusetts, just over the New Hampshire border.

My parents went to the Episcopal Church of the Good Shepherd in Nashua. My father's mother (Frances) was very active in the church guild and was the "choir mother." My father was an acolyte and choir member in the boys' and men's choir for years. My parents were married in that church and lived in Nashua until moving to New Britain (Corbin Avenue) around 1935—1936.

I don't remember much about living in Nashua but I do recall my father talking about learning to swim in the Merrimac River and playing baseball with "Birdie" Tebbetts, a famous Boston Red Sox catcher. My father was also a catcher and had the bent little fingers to prove it. My parents also talked about "blueberrying" in the Hudson, and getting flooded out in the great flood of the 1930s.

Nashua was like a big "small town," and until I was seven or eight years old I was more familiar with Nashua than I was with New Britain. We visited Nashua often, staying with Grammy McCain at 2 Temple Place, Nashua. Seems like everybody knew "Curly" (my father) and my mother. Like many towns, Nashua was divided into "ethnic" sections. Richard, David, and I could wander all around the city, stores, movie theater, and playground. It seems like everyone knew we were Curly's boys and were watched out for. Occasionally we were told we were wandering too far into some sections of town and to go back the other way. Grammy always made delicious homemade cinnamon sugar donuts for us.

Like many people of that era, my father left school after graduating from the eighth grade. I don't know much about that time of his life but I do know that at that time it was common for young men to start "earning a living."

I deeply regret not knowing more about him. I've seen pictures of him in an Army uniform, dressed as a choir boy and an acolyte in church, on a motorcycle with a side car (as a lad he used to visit his Uncle Arthur Ord in Cookshire, Canada), in a baseball uniform (he was noted for his athletic ability in Nashua), and in pictures of him and Mom at Hampton Beach.

I've also been told that he was a "cooper" (someone who makes wooden buckets and barrels) or apprenticed to one. He left that for the foundry (non-ferrous) trade, became a skilled molder, cove maker, and eventually foreman in Nashua. In the mid-1930s, Tuttle and Bailey of New Britain bought the New Hampshire Foundry and moved it to New Britain. A number of the New Hampshire men moved to New Britain with the job, my father and Uncle George among them. The McCain family relocated to Corbin Avenue, New Britain.

My mother was a very attractive lady, well built, with fair skin, blue-gray eyes and long, black, silky hair. After high school, I believe she worked at the Card Shop (I think it was a factory in Nashua) before she was married. I remember her as being well read, knew all about the Bible (occasionally referred to me as Nicodemus), was a great student of English and literature, and claimed to be somehow related to Noah Webster. She was also, like many women of her era, an expert in all kinds of needlework, sewing, gardening, cooking, etc.

Mother was very wise and ahead of her time and something to be reckoned with. She was also very caring and had many friends. Most of all, from my perspective, she was a great mother and teacher and a perfect match for my father. He was a hard working sensitive man, a quiet leader, who was respected and liked by everybody. The sort of man that others, and I, tried to emulate, the kind of man that Rudyard Kipling wrote about.

I have never outgrown wanting to be near and dear to my parents. I'm proud of them and I miss them. Their presence made this world a little better for a lot of people.

Chapter 4: Early School and Growing Up

Back in New Britain, in September 1943, I left Israel Putnam Elementary School, where I had come to feeling quite comfortable and was a good student. I had skipped a grade, so I was younger than most of my classmates but physically matched up very well. My new school was Washington Junior High School, a little further from home and in a "tougher" part of the city. The older kids picked on us "new" kids and on one of the first days some of them got me on the way to school and tied me to a tree. It was a while before I got loose and of course, I was late for school, embarrassed, scared, and mad. The move to Kensington was great for me. The move let me start over and reset the way classmates thought of me.

Growing up in Connecticut, we definitely had seasons. Learning to ice skate on the many ponds in the area, sometimes the older kids and parents would shovel off large areas of the pond and skate at night and have a big bonfire. Before the ice got thick enough, we kids (without parents' knowledge) would go to the shallow ends and play "dare" on the "rubber ice" (that's ice that's so thin that if you got on it and stayed still you'd fall through, but if you moved fast enough it would bend and crack but you could make it across). Of course, when you fell in you got wet and sometimes it was so cold that by the time you got home and got your pants off by the stove in the kitchen, they were frozen and would stand alone. We also went coasting (sliding) using anything imaginable: pieces of cardboard, homemade coasters from barrel staves, etc. If you were really lucky you had a "flexible flyer" sled. We also would actually go sledding on the roads. They were never sanded and there was very little traffic, and the buses and cars and trucks used chains on their tires so there was no salt or sand to slow you down.

I also remember the time we went sledding by the convent, where there was an exceptionally good hill. At the top of the hill was an iron fence and one of the kids dared me to put my tongue on the fence. I did, and it got stuck. David had to go home and get my mother, who came back with a tea kettle of hot water to unstick me. Several lessons learned there!

Spring was a love-hate thing with me. It brought on my annual and inevitable bout with poison ivy. I would swell up—hands, face, all over my body, and itch terribly. For a couple of weeks, it was calamine lotion, compresses, and yellow soap. There were areas near the bunk where I scratched through the wallpaper and plaster to the lathe work. Later, in my early teens this severe reaction to poison ivy was relieved by getting shots. I can still get poison ivy but now in a normal sense.

The good part about spring is that everything is starting up again. The farmers are planting, the animals are out of the barn, and everything is new. A good time to start over. The days got longer, the weather warmer, and school let out. Time to explore and do new things. Summer seemed to last a lot longer then.

In New Britain, we used to hike up to Pinnacle Rock. We also hiked Rattlesnake Mountain, which overlooks the old town of Farmington, to a boulder cave called "Bill Warren's Den." Legend had it that in the early colonial days a local citizen named Bill Warren had all of his property and livestock confiscated in Farmington for not paying his taxes. To get even, he set fire to it all and fled to a cave on the mountain where Indians hid him out. Nearby the cave was a sassafras bush. We used to cut twigs from it and chew the ends for the taste like the Indians did. When they dried they were a handy toothbrush. The farmers all seemed to chew snuff and either in their bib or rear pocket there was the faded ring imprint of their snuff can. We tried to get that look too but we put cow mash (coarse corn flour) in our snuff cans. In retrospect, much of what we did was an attempt to emulate the grownups and to become "grown up."

Summers in Kensington were different in that there was no farm, no livestock, no planting, and no harvesting—more suburban-like. However, there was plenty to do: Boy Scouts, camps, church, World War II activities, paper route, and a much wider circle of friends. A dozen or so of us got together and formed an athletic group called the "Kensington Raiders." Mostly it was football, baseball, and ice hockey. We challenged and played against other teams from Berlin, East Berlin, and New Britain. I would say the age group was between 12 and 16 years old. There were no "little leagues" at that time, and by 16 kids were either playing high school sports or working.

It was also at this time that I got much more

involved in church activities (I was an acolyte for years), the Boy Scouts (I was in the "Order of the Arrow"), war effort activities (scrap drives, rationing, black-outs, fire brigade, etc.), camping (I had a pup tent and gear and would go off by myself for a few days at a time), high school sports, and a girlfriend who I loved dearly.

Chapter 5: War Effects

The War was a big influence on our lives in many ways. In schools we had regular "air raid drills" along with the regular "fire drills." In an "air raid drill" you dropped to the floor and got under your desk or table. In a "fire drill," you and the class assembled outside of the building at an assigned area. At night, all outside windows of houses and buildings had to be sealed so that no light could be seen from the outside. Street lights were turned off and all automobiles and trucks had the top half of their headlights painted black (this was to prevent the submarines from being able to silhouette ships to torpedo off the Connecticut coast).

Part I. Dad's Words

Young men were being drafted into the services and many weren't waiting but were enlisting. It was common to see houses with 8 ½ by 11-inch blue flags with a white star centered in it hanging in a window. That meant that a person from that house was in the service. A flag with a gold star meant that the person had been killed. (For instance, the McAdoos had three white stars and one gold). Younger boys and others not eligible for the service were organized to become air raid wardens, airplane spotters, fire brigaders, etc.

Many things were hard to get or were rationed. Each household received its allotted ration book of stamps for such things as sugar, meat, coffee, gasoline, oil, etc.

I remember having to bring some ration stamps when I went to Boy Scout camp. I really liked camping and would go often; it was a nice "get away" and time for reflection. Clearly, my growing up was accelerated during these years.

Chapter 6: Memories of My Parents and Life Lessons Learned

My father, Francis Albert McCain, was born 12 November 1902 and died 29 November 1974. He was approximately 5' 11" tall, had brown curly hair, brown eyes, weighed approximately 190 pounds, was well built and known as Curly to everyone except for us boys who called him Dad. In looks and mannerisms he was much like John Wayne. My mother, Irene Teresa Lucier McCain, was born 18 May 1898 and died 20 August 1980. She was approximately 5' 6" tall, had black hair, gray-green eyes, was well built and attractive, and everyone called her Irene except for us boys who called her Mom.

Of the two, I would say that Mom was the major disciplinarian in everyday matters and was totally backed up by my father. There was no playing one against the other for us kids.

Generally, "discipline" was administered by a stern word or look, followed by the reason why. Occasionally, it meant the temporary loss of a privilege and, rarely, a whack with a switch. I can't remember ever being punished for doing something that I didn't know or should have known to be wrong. Not that we were angels, but in retrospect it meant that we got caught doing something worth the calculated risk.

In retrospect, let me draw this analogy: it is natural and normal for a parent to be protective. It is natural and normal for a person to explore his or her world. I experienced all of that. As a baby, the child is placed in a crib for safety and exploration. When the baby has thoroughly explored the crib and outgrown it, they're placed in a playpen. Outgrowing the playpen, they're placed in a child-safe room and, eventually, the house, yard, community, etc.—all the time learning and exploring and growing and developing, with confidence, to assume their roles in family and society. Always feeling safe and secure in their own knowledge of the present environment and yet expanding their growth through exploring their own parameters.

As mentioned earlier, my parents met and married in Nashua, New Hampshire, sometime around 1925. They had their first son, Robert, who died shortly after Richard was born in 1928. Then came me, David, and Thomas. I'm sure it wasn't easy for them. Their first home was lost to the great flood in Nashua. The timing was the beginning of the Great Depression and to follow the work they moved to Connecticut, accompanied by the food shortages and then the wars. Daunting and challenging times for sure, but we never felt it to be gloomy or destructive.

Both my parents were very self-reliant and they conscientiously tried to pass those qualities on to each of us along with, by example, teaching us to respect ourselves and others. Some examples: "Would you like to be stuck on a deserted island with someone like that?"; "You divide it, they get first choice"; "A penny saved is a penny earned"; Kipling's poem "IF"; household chores; Sunday school; "A job worth doing is worth doing well"; "If you don't like yourself, neither can anyone else"; "Do unto others as you would have them do unto you"; "Waste not, want not"; "A stitch in time saves nine"; "As the twig is bent, so grows the tree"; and more of such adages garnered from a variety of sources like *Poor Richard's Almanac,* Yankee folklore, the Bible, classic literature and such.

We were read to and encouraged to read. Along with the standard family collection of the Bible, Encyclopedia Britannica (which was updated annually with the latest edition), and dictionary, I remember my mother's leather-bound collection of literary classics—a set of about 20 books inscribed as given to her, Irene Teresa Lucier, in 1907 (unfortunately they were lost in the fire of Tim's house in Natick, Massachusetts, in the mid-1990s). We also had magazine subscriptions such as *Popular Mechanics, Saturday Evening Post,* and *Boys' Life.* My father was a big Zane Grey fan. So, as a household we ran the gamut, all the way from comics on to serious literature.

Imagine daily life without TV, cell phones, Facebook, texting, etc. Our daily activities involved learning how to listen and learn, converse and teach, and develop and use our imagination. Chores made us part of the group, which was satisfying for us and helpful to the rest.

Both of my parents were very talented in many ways. And, if one were to be trapped on a deserted island, either or both would be ideal companions. They both were optimistic, supportive, and creative, and between them it seemed that anything could be fixed, mended, repaired, created, or resolved. We were taught to be handy with tools and equipment, to sew, cook, garden, etc., as well as how to deal with problems and adversity. Examples: One day, when we boys were all quite young, we were on a motoring trip visiting the White Mountains in New Hampshire. The scenery and sights were quite wonderful. While descending one steep hill, looking ahead the road loomed up and over us, so high, so steep, so scary, that one of us said, "Stop, don't go up, we'll fall off the world." My mother said, "Boys, don't worry and watch carefully; this big hill is just like other problems you will face in life. We will continue on, face it, and get over it. It's nowhere near as bad as you think." And, sure enough, as we came down our side of the hill, the road ahead seemed to flatten out and was nowhere near as threatening or scary as it first seemed. And at the top, there was nothing to fall off of. Another lesson learned....

Flashing way ahead in time...I had just turned sixteen, thought I knew everything and could do anything. I wanted to be "on my own." That night at supper I announced my plans: to quit school, get a job, and move out. I was expecting a calamity to occur, but no, instead my parents asked if we could talk about it in detail the next night. I agreed, thinking I had made my point. The next night, my parents started off by saying how proud of me they were. That I had grown up so fast, and was all ready to assume the responsibilities that go along with being "grown up."

My father said I could get a full-time job at the foundry as a laborer and what the pay would be. My mother told me of two places she had found where I could stay and their costs. One was room and board and the other room only. However, they made it clear that they preferred I remain at home and the cost for room and board would be very competitive. And, finally, they made the offer that so long as I stayed successfully in school, I could live at home without cost. It didn't take long for me to figure out two things: one, that at the end of the week I would have more "pocket money" by staying in school and at home, continuing my part-time jobs, and, two, being "grown up" isn't only defined as being just a big, smart, wise guy. Another lesson learned...

Chapter 7: Money

My parents didn't talk about money a lot or dwell on it a lot. But, we were taught to respect money as being important and not to be wasted. We weren't given allowances for doing chores like a lot of other kids were, but could earn money by doing some "extras." I don't remember ever feeling deprived, envious, or poor with one exception. I remember as a kid thinking how wonderful it must be to be so rich that one could always have enough candy in his pocket so that he could carry it around and not eat it all immediately. To this day, I still almost always have some mints or candy in my pocket.

I also remember, as a boy, being so shy that when my mother and I were out doing errands and would meet somebody I would hide behind her dress. Then one day she wrote a note and pinned it with some money to my underwear, and sent me alone to the insurance man's office with the payment. It made me feel big, proud, brave, and trusted. And, of course, another lesson learned.

Chapter 8: Education and Religion

As mentioned, at home we were encouraged to read, explore, and get involved in our own interests. In school it was quite clear that my parents were much more concerned with the assessment of our effort and decorum marks than with grades (a wise move, I thought, for character development).

Richard did not go to college, but in the Army was sent to motor repair school and in civilian life he was a mechanic, owned his own gas station and garage, and then became the head mechanic of a major trucking firm.

I eventually went to college, earned a BA in education and a master's in education. I taught school and worked for the CEA (Connecticut Education Association).

David went to college, earned a BA, ME, and PhD, taught school and became a junior high school principal.

Thomas went to college, earned a BA, MA, and PhD, taught school, became a principal, and then a superintendent of schools.

The Episcopal Church of the Good Shepherd in Nashua is where I and all of my brothers, except Tom, were baptized. Thomas was baptized in St. Mark's Episcopal Church in New Britain, Connecticut.

My father sang in both the boys' choir and the men's choir at the Good Shepherd. His mother, Frances McCain, was in the Lady's Guild and the "choir mother" there. Richard, Thomas, and I were acolytes at St. Mark's for many years. We were all communicants and attended church, Sunday school, and other church activities regularly. Also, my mother made the baptismal dress for each of us boys. Mine was used again when each of my two boys—David and Timothy—were baptized. Tim has it now, having used it for his two children, Christopher and Courtney.

Chapter 9: Family Activities

Birthdays. Your birthday started from the time that you got up, not when it was convenient for somebody else. If you had a school day or work day you had your choice of a favorite breakfast before you went off. But at suppertime it was important that everyone be there and share your favorite meal, followed by cake and presents. It was a show of respect for you.

Vacations. Most often spent together as a family and often as guests to relatives or close friends, who, in turn, would be our guests later. That meant frequent visits to New Hampshire, Maine, and Canada. I remember a lot of happy times playing in the sand and waves at Hampton Beach, Salisbury Beach, and York Beach, as well as very fond memories of the Ord homestead farm in Cookshire, Canada.

Chapter 10: Holidays

Christmas was big in our house. Everyone had a stocking hung on the mantle, hoping to catch an orange or tangerine and a piece of candy. The tree was in the corner of the room, well decorated with some very fancy and delicate glass ornaments, but mostly with homemade colored paper chains, popcorn chains, stars, bells, trinkets, and a lot of tinsel. Underneath, gifts were brightly wrapped and labeled "not to be opened before Christmas morning." This also meant don't get caught lifting them, jiggling them, handling them, or squeezing them. We had no trouble going to bed on time on Christmas Eve; our trouble was going to sleep. Eventually we did and it seemed that usually closer to four a.m. than six a.m. one of us would wake, rouse the others, and joyously bound into our parents' bedroom to rouse them and get them down to the fun of opening presents. I remember at least once being talked into going back to bed after opening the presents to finish our night's sleep.

Chapter 11: Brothers

There were five McCain brothers: Robert, Richard, Russell, David, and Thomas.

Robert Henry McCain, born November 20, 1925, died April 28, 1931, at the age of five. Robert, I do not remember, as I was an infant when he passed. I have seen some early photos but that is the extent of my knowledge. He is buried in the family plot at the Hillside Cemetery, Nashua, New Hampshire.

Richard Ord McCain, born January 24, 1928, died May 12, 1982, at the age of 54. Richard died unexpectedly from cancer after a very short illness at an early age. Growing up, he was the oldest of us boys. He was three years older than I and that was quite a difference as kids. Being the oldest, he was the first in a lot of things, like going to school, getting to wear long pants instead of knickers and knee socks, being an acolyte, and driving a car. But being the first wasn't all that great either; it means to me that it carried higher expectations, usually, and often more scrutiny and responsibility. In some ways he was sort of a trailblazer for the rest of us. Richard was smart, a quick learner and hard worker. He got along well with adults and was mechanically inclined. Thus, as a boy, he got to do a lot more of the things around the farm than the rest of us kids, such as running the hay-rake and helping with repairs. Also, while in high school, he got a job repairing and rebuilding automobile engines, and later owned his own service station.

One thing we did tease him about though, he was a lefty. In high school, he was a pretty good pitcher, but his hand-me-down gloves were of no use to me, not being left handed. David, however, gobbled them up as he was a lefty too, and a good one. Poor Tom. We, his older brothers, would argue as we taught him to catch, throw, and kick—both right and left. To this day I still don't think he knows if he is a righty or a lefty.

Anyway, as kids, Richard was fun to play with. We made our own pea-shooters, slingshots, rubber band games, kites, and even our own "pop" guns (a little vinegar in the bottom of a coke bottle, a teaspoon of baking soda wrapped in toilet paper carefully wedged in the neck of the bottle, and plugged with a cork, fairly tight; shake the bottle well and wait for the "pop").

As we got into senior high school, Richard's world grew, as did his group of friends. I think I was still in high school when he got drafted into the Army. Not too soon after he got out of the Army, he married Doris Button. I was the best man. I am also the godfather to his first child, Brian McCain. Brian was followed by Doreen, Lynn, and Laura, who are all married and living in Connecticut with children of their own. Richard's wife, Doris, remarried after his passing to Edwin McAdoo, a widower.

David Winthrop McCain, born September 11, 1933, died June 23, 2004, at the age of 70. David died after a fairly long struggle with cancer. He was sixteen months younger than me, and my closest-aged mate. Even as kids, he was a big boy and about the same size as Richard and me. So, in our house, we boys were "color coded" to keep the peace when it came to clothing (shirts, socks, mittens, sweaters, etc.). Richard was black and blue, I was green and brown, and David was maroon and light blue. The color coding resolved many problems about such things as who hadn't put their clothes away, whose scarf do you have on, who lost a mitten, etc.

Although as kids we three were relatively the same size, we did differ in many ways. Richard was three years ahead of me in school and I was two years ahead of David. Richard was fascinated by mechanics and engineering. I liked nature, scouting, and working with my hands, while David liked people, kids, and exploring. But, as kids and brothers, we three got along very well. If anything, we picked on David a little too often because he was for the most part a big willing target and glad to be included. But, every once in a while, he would let us know when we went too far. For example, one of the toys we had was a red wagon, with wooden sideboards that could be added to carry bigger items like bags of hay. Well, we used to make believe that it was a runaway stagecoach, and the wagon puller would race around the yard, trying to tip over the wagon and driver. One day, I was the driver and David was the horse. To be realistic, I insisted that he put a rope in his mouth that I would use like reins to steer "the horse." When he started pulling, I yanked on the reins to steer him. He just ran faster. I pulled back and forth, harder and harder, until his mouth bled. He just kept running faster and faster straight over to the shed where a rake was leaning against the wall. He grabbed the rake, turned around, and wacked me on the top of the head. I still feel those bumps today! It was a bloody sight.

David was good athlete. In high school he was a star pitcher—lefty of course—and a football player, a lineman. He was also an excellent swimmer and, from age 16 on through college, was a life guard at the municipal swimming pool in Berlin.

In college, David was a star pitcher on the baseball team and a starting tackle on the football team. He was invited to try out for at least two professional baseball teams that I know of and to attend the Cleveland Rams training camp in football. When I asked why he didn't accept any invitations, he said he played because he liked it, but to turn pro it would be work, not fun, and he would have to give up too much.

After high school, David went to Central Connecticut State University, became an elementary school teacher in Newington, Connecticut, earned a master's degree and doctorate degree, became the principal of the Newington middle school, and was awarded the "Principal of the Year" by the Connecticut State Department of Education.

David was also drafted into the Army (1957 to 1959), did his basic training at Fort Dix, New Jersey, was awarded the "outstanding soldier" award of the boot camp cycle, and spent the remainder of his time in the Army at Camp Zama in Japan.

After he got out of the Army, he married Diane, a school teacher. I was the best man at his wedding. They had a daughter, Heather, and a son, Clark. Clark is now married and has a family of his own, as does Heather. Diane and David divorced and David remarried Cheryl, another school teacher, who had two sons, Brian and Jonathan, both of whom are now married and have families.

After the Army, David also found time to get a pilot's license and enjoyed flying around the state of Connecticut and taking day trips to Cape Cod and such. Sarah wasn't keen on me flying with him, although I sometimes did and we dreamed about taking flying trips to Canada and Alaska for remote fishing adventures. I miss him....

Thomas George McCain, born October 18, 1937. Thomas is almost six years younger than me, born in October 1937 in New Britain. He was the only one of us boys not born in a hospital. He was born at home, 469 Osgood Avenue. I remember it being late afternoon, early evening, the doctor arriving at the house, we boys being shooed into our bedrooms and told to stay out of the way, a flurry of hustling around, some noise and commotion, and then an overwhelming smell making its way through the house: ether. Then, happy noise and we were told we had another brother. A while later I saw my father go out back with a pail and shovel (I later learned it was to bury the placenta). We were glad he was a boy; we understood boys; we knew he would fit right in.

In the beginning, Tommy was better than a new toy. We all liked to hold him, play with his little fingers and toes, create reactions and ask my mother all kinds of questions. As he developed our activities changed. We spent our time showing him how to walk, tumble, talk, throw, kick, and play games. Sometimes I'm sure it was most confusing to him because Richard and David were left-handed and I was right-handed. In many activities, he was drilled in both ways, lefty and righty, before making a choice. Even now, if you were to watch him go through a full day of activities, you would be confused as to whether he was a righty or lefty.

By the time we moved to Kensington in 1943, Tom was just starting public school, David was in elementary school, I was in seventh grade, and Richard was in high school. We were developing our own groups of friends and interests. I mention this now because it was much later that Tom and David turned things around for me and were of great help to me.

Part I. Dad's Words

Tom was a much more knowledgeable and better public student than I. In 1950, Tommy was a freshman in high school; I, a freshman in college (along with David, who had just graduated from high school). I got there because I was a good football player, as opposed to being a good student.

The program for the Teachers College of Connecticut (now known as Central Connecticut State University) required that for the first two years everybody took essentially the same courses. At the end of the two years, you had to apply to the college for readmission. If you got accepted to the college, you then had to apply to the department of your major discipline (i.e., math, history, science, elementary education, industrial arts, etc.). Obviously, in the beginning I didn't have a clue about some of my subjects like math, algebra, and science. So, I turned to Tommy. He helped me every night with my homework and became my tutor, teaching me how to study and what to study, to the point that at the end of my sophomore year, when I applied for readmission to the Teachers College, I was awarded "outstanding male sophomore" and given a scholarship for my junior and senior years. I majored in Industrial Arts. David chose to major in Elementary Education.

Tom graduated from high school the year I graduated from college. Tom also went to Central Connecticut Teachers College, majored in Elementary Education, taught school in Connecticut, earned a master's degree and doctorate degree, and became a principal and Superintendent of Schools in New Jersey.

In 1959 Tom married Sandra Kevorkian, who was a fellow parishioner at St. Mark's Church. I was the best man.

Tom and Sandra wanted children and soon adopted a baby girl, Jodi Beth, who was and is a pride and joy, is now married and the mother of two delightful girls. Shortly after Jodi Beth came along, Sandra gave birth to a son, Scott, who is also now a married father and an additional pride and joy for Tom and Sandra in their retirement years. Tom and Sandra currently reside in Hendersonville, North Carolina.

Chapter 12: Entertainment

When we lived on Osgood Avenue, we three older boys were allowed occasionally (about once a month) to take the bus into the city of New Britain and go to the movies—total cost, 25 cents each. The bus had a big glass coin box that you dropped your money into. We were the last stop on the line and it cost seven cents each way. The bus driver had a coin dispenser to make change if you needed it. The movie theater cost 11 cents and when you went in, you got a free "Eskimo Pie" ice cream bar. On the way out you got a free carnival glass dish or plate or other part of a set of dishes. Our set was sort of a clear rose-pink shade, which we used at home. The movies always started with "coming attractions," "advertisements," "news reels," and then, two movies. Total time, about four to four-and-one-half hours.

Sunday afternoons, if the weather was good, were spent "going for a ride" in the car, usually sightseeing, or to some park or zoo. Or, sometimes, just exploring, and then home in time to listen to the Sunday evening radio programs.

Chapter 13: Jobs

I believe it was the summer between sixth and seventh grade that I planned to become self-employed and make some money. I noticed some kids with shoe-shine boxes getting paid to shine other people's shoes. I watched them for a while and then went home and began building my own shoe-shine box. It was a beauty. I even added a shoulder strap to carry it. I borrowed some money for polish, a brush, and rags, and went back to the center of town and set up shop right in front of the biggest bank in the city. Before long, two bigger kids came along, banged me up, and smashed my box. I called a cop. He told me I was lucky he didn't give me a ticket because I didn't have a permit. Then he said if I ever did get one I couldn't set up there because I would have to earn my way to a good spot.

That winter we moved to Berlin, and I started a paper route with three customers. But, as more and more people moved into the development it grew to a very nice number of 50 to 60 customers, six days a week.

Part I. Dad's Words

My next "paying" job was with the Berlin Railroad Station. It was winter work, part-time snow shoveling. It required having a Social Security number and being at least 16 years old. At the time I was only 14 years old, so I used my brother Richard's birthdate (January 24, 1928) on the application form. I got the job and a Social Security card with numbers that were different than most others. I was told that it was because the railroad was country-wide coded and not regionally coded like most other places. The job was easy: we were to keep the station platform clean of snow around the clock, because it was a very busy station. I worked nights and it seemed to snow a lot of nights that winter. Between shoveling we would catch naps on the benches in the station. Of course we would only work when there were snow storms. That Social Security number would cause some problems later in life.

The next winter I got a better paying part-time job with the Connecticut State Highway Department working during snow storms. It was on a plow and salt spreader truck assigned to Route 44, from West Hartford through Farmington, Simsbury, Avon, Canton, and to New Hartford. We had one mission: when it was snowing hard, we were plowing. My job was to raise and lower the plow when crossing railroad tracks, culverts, and such. When the snowfall dwindled or stopped, I got in back of the truck and cut open sacks of salt to pour on the road. The driver was a nice guy, not much of a talker, a native Indian, who drove with his window open, keeping the cab quite cold. At times he would have snow in his lap and I would have the heater aimed full blast at me. It was a good job though, and when we stopped for meals the state would pay.

For three years in high school I was a "volunteer firefighter cadet." Several of us volunteered for this because it was a good way to get out of school and for excitement, especially in the spring. We never tended to any houses, mainly brush fires, grass fires and once, a dump. Every once in a while the Volunteer Fire Department would call the school, come pick us up, and we'd go off like heroes. Our tools were a rake, shovel, an

Indian pump water tank, and we'd help get the fire under control. We had a ball and they were grateful—good deal!

The last paying job I had while in high school was at Eddie's Diner. It was the classic railroad car-style diner, next to the Berlin Railroad Station and near the high school. I worked there on the counter weekday mornings and a half-day on Saturday. Weekdays I got there before 6 a.m. and left by 8 a.m. Saturday was 6 a.m. to 11 a.m.

When I graduated from high school, I went to work in the foundry. It was fascinating and challenging and demanding and, sure enough, I started at the bottom. A foundry is a place where they melt metal and pour it into different shapes. Non-ferrous meant that we worked with metals other than iron (i.e., copper, brass, aluminum, bronze, etc.). Foundry work is hot, dirty, smoky, and noisy. One spends most of the day soaking wet in sweat. Metal castings are made by molding, tamping sand around an object, and then removing the pattern and filling the void (mold) with molten metal. In the beginning, I spent most of my time shifting weights, dumping molds, and shoveling sand, i.e., grunt work. From there I went to core making. A core is made from very fine sand, mixed with a binder, and formed in a metal mold, much in the way a casting is formed in a sand mold. The core is then baked in an oven until it hardens. Then it can be handled without breaking and placed inside the sand mold before the molten metal is poured in, to make something hollow—for example, a salt shaker. From there, I got into molding, both "machine" and "loose work"; machine being mass production work, and loose work meaning individual pieces, like plaques, door plates, sculptures, toys, etc.

The environment was demanding. It required a range of physical needs, from brute strength to a delicate touch, and it was challenging. Pouring molten metal into the spew hole in a block of sand to make a casting was fascinating. I admired my father, my Uncle George, the McAdoo boys, and everybody who worked at the McAdoo Foundry.

Part I. Dad's Words

As I mentioned before, the foundry was brought to Connecticut from New Hampshire sometime during the 1930s by Tuttle and Bailey; thus, we moved to Connecticut. Early in the 1940s Tuttle and Bailey decided to replace the part of its factory that housed the foundry by expanding the machine shop. My father and Uncle George, along with some others who came with the foundry from New Hampshire, were offered similar paying jobs in other parts of the shop. Some took them, some didn't. Also, they offered the foundry machines, equipment, and materials instead of a job. Uncle George, Dad, and I don't know if anybody else was initially involved, started up the McAdoo Foundry, and were later joined by Olin, Paul and Edwin McAdoo, and Richard McCain, who had to quit because of zinc poisoning from the fumes. I started full time after graduating from high school.

Now I was definitely a man, doing a man's work and making a man's wage, and getting good at it. But then one day I looked around —there were no middle-aged guys in the foundry except for my Dad and Uncle, and a couple of sad "hanger on-ers."

I began to look around and wonder what I would be doing in 30 or 40 years. My brother David already said he was going to college. No way was I prepared for that—but I could play football. I was already playing at a semi-pro level and getting paid (once as much as a whole week's salary in the foundry).

One morning, on the ride to work with my father, I mentioned that I was thinking about going to college.

"Great," my Father said. "Are you planning on studying metallurgy or business?" He was thinking of the future of the foundry.

"Not really," I replied. "I was thinking of working with people instead of things."

Silence—a long silence—and I slowly began to realize how I must have hurt him, the man I admired most and wished I could be as good as!

"Okay," he said, breaking the silence and picking up on my growing discomfort. "I understand and know that if every day an alarm clock is needed to get you off to work, you've got the wrong job."

It was then that I made a silent promise to myself and him that I would continue as much as possible to work with him in the foundry in the future and that he would be proud of my success in whatever career I ended up in.

Chapter 14: Football and College

Through my semi-pro football connection, I got a scholarship to a small college in Kentucky, now known as Moorhead State. I went there for one fall. It was not a good experience, and I came home.

("It was not a good experience and I came home." These are the only words my Dad wrote about his football experience at Moorhead State. He told me, on the other hand, many stories about this time in his life. I will retell here only the ones that he did not specifically instruct me not to repeat. At the age of 18, my Dad was told he had a full college scholarship in exchange for his playing football at Moorhead State in

Kentucky. He was told he would be the starting guard on the offensive line, even though only a freshman. In early July 1949, he made his way to the Berlin train station lugging a metal trunk locker, boarded a train, and took the 20-hour ride to Kentucky. On the first day of practice, there was a bit of "confusion" as he called it. You see, my Dad and 30 other freshmen were each told they would be a "starter" on the football team. Trouble was that between the freshmen, sophomore, junior, and senior classes, there were over 100 players on the field. The way my Dad told it, he would always begin, "Imagine this: an old, grizzled coach in a worn baseball cap, gray tee-shirt and sweat pants, climbs an old, rickety wooden tower with a megaphone in his hands, just like a 1940s black-and-white movie." To which I would always remind him, "Dad, it was the 1940s." He would then continue: "The coach brings the megaphone up and shouts, 'Now listen, I don't care if you're a freshman or a senior. I don't care if you started last year or just got here. We're gonna practice here for six weeks. And after those six weeks, the best 30 of ya can stay here and play football, and the rest of ya can get the heck outta here and go back to your mommas and your sisters.'" As my Dad explained it, "The blood and the fur flew." Dad made the football team and started on the offensive line. When he was back home for Christmas break, he received his grades. "Three C's and two B's," he would say, "and I never saw the inside of a classroom." He also used to tell that, "I got paid, too, cash, every week for my job, which was raking the leaves off of the football field." Usually I would ask, "Dad, the football field had trees on it?" to which he would simply smile, shrug his shoulders, and raise his hands. He did not return for a second semester.)

With more help from the semi-pro team connections, I got into the New Britain State Teachers College, now known as Central Connecticut State University, and started out as a freshman with my brother David.

So there I was one hot August day, reporting for practice with the Teachers College of Connecticut's football team and grateful to be there. One of the first things I noticed was that practically everybody else on the team (except David and me) was a veteran who had already served his time in the military services. The same held true for most of the student body. Guys were beginning or resuming their college careers with the help of the G.I. Bill (financial aid for returning veterans). They were older, wiser, and more serious in what they were doing and why they were doing it. It was a good example to follow.

Football went well. I made the starting team as a freshman, as well as sophomore, junior, and senior years. In addition, I co-captained the last three years, was "Most Valuable Player" senior year, and All State New England Honorable Mention. Also, because of my workload, in the fall of each year I took one less course; thus I had a semester to make up in the fifth year. Traditionally, we had a head coach, line coach, and backfield coach. Just prior to the season of my fifth year we lost the head coach, so our line coach took that position and the college hired me as the line coach. That year we had the first undefeated season in the school's history.

Studies demanded a lot of effort but went well with the aforementioned help of Tom, David, home, and valued friends. I did not live on campus, but rather commuted from home. So, in a sense, it was like continuing on high school, except with a purpose (and in my case, harder). Usually, I would go into the foundry in the morning, use those early hours to study, go to school, and then stop back at the foundry to do a little work (like mixing core sand), and then home. Holidays and vacations were spent at the foundry. This kept me in pocket money.

Chapter 15: The Army

During this time, I had a major concern: I was so close to the end and did not want to get drafted and break my stride. I wanted to graduate. Many schools had an ROTC program but Teachers College did not. However, I did hear about a "draft deferment test": if you took this test and achieved a certain grade or better and if you were in an upper percentile of your class, then a statement of confirmation from the school with a written request for deferment would get you a semester's deferment from the draft. This process had to be repeated each semester.

I took the test, filled out the forms, made the request, and hand delivered it to the draft board. Wow! What a surprise. The "draft board" turned out to be a beautiful, personable, and confident blonde, who became even more attractive as she explained the procedures to me. Her name was Sarah Villecco, and I began to look forward to the beginning of each new semester as an excuse to see her. Then one Saturday night I went out with some guys from school and we stopped in at a dance where Sarah and some of her friends were. I ended up spending most of the evening with her and drove her home.

After that evening we started dating. Finally, only one semester to go before graduation, I was ready for student teaching. Fortunately, I was offered a full-time job teaching woodworking in Warwick, Rhode Island. That meant that not only would I get paid but I would have a year's teaching experience and my obligation of student teaching would be fulfilled.

Part I. Dad's Words

I had a room in Rhode Island, would leave Connecticut Monday morning, return Friday evening, and saw Sarah every weekend. By now I was feeling pretty good; the school year was about over; summer was just around the corner; and all was well with Sarah. I was only months away from another birthday, my 25th, which would take me out of the "one-A" draft status. Then, one early weekend in June, when I picked up Sarah she asked if I had received any mail. "Why?" I asked. It came the next day: my draft notice. I was to report to Fort Dix, July 5, 1955. I was drafted.

I Love You Dad

Part II. My Honor

Chapter 16: I Was Drafted

I was drafted.

We are all drafted. God has a plan for all of us. My Dad was drafted into the Army. I was drafted to finish and write this book, to finish my Dad's story. I was drafted to describe the love of a father and son. I was drafted to write about a three-day journey, a journey that changed and bettered my life forever. I was drafted to describe how seemingly simple, everyday chores create the most impactful and lasting memories. I was drafted to share my love of my Dad with all of you.

"I was drafted," my Dad's last written contribution to this story, occurred in late March 2012. His next contributions would be his greatest, though, sadly, he never read about them. His next contributions were of heroics, strength, and the will to keep order. His next contribution was the consistent lesson that family matters and that humility is strength. Let me fulfill my drafted duty and share my Dad's last contributions to his story with you. Allow me to draft your attention for thirty minutes and tell you about The Drive.

Chapter 17: The Drive

On April 15, 2012, I began the three most incredibly emotional and difficult days of my life. Here I sit, as I write, some five months later, and this mere half sentence, coupled with the thought of those three days, brings tears and emotion unlike any I could ever conceivably describe. My memory of The Drive still paralyzes me and reduces me to a quivering, tear-filled child; yet, I am 51 years old.

You see, every year for the last 25 or so, my parents, and my aunt and my uncle (my incredible and beloved godparents Uncle George and Auntie Mary) have driven down to south Florida, Hallandale in particular, from their homes in Bristol, Connecticut.

My Uncle George passed early, in 1992, at the age of 61, his lungs ravaged by a career working with asbestos. I still miss him and think about him almost daily, especially lately in a happy and gentle way because I know he is smiling at my youngest son, Danny, entering the University of Notre Dame as a freshman, and Notre Dame was Uncle George's favorite school.

This year, 2012, like the many others that preceded it, my Dad, Mom, and Auntie Mary drove south to Hallandale in mid-January. Their drives are always accompanied by some comical misadventure, such as the time my Dad drove down after recently undergoing knee replacement surgery on his right knee, his driving leg. I remember my Mom calling to tell me, "Dad ran a stop sign."

"Oh," I replied, "he didn't see it?"

"No," she said, "I mean he ran over the stop sign because he couldn't stop, because he couldn't lift his foot off of the accelerator with his hands until I leaned over to help him."

"What?!" I said.

"Yes" she said. "You see, he has some nerve damage from the knee replacement surgery that I'm sure is temporary, but it prevents him from lifting his foot. So, he can press down on the accelerator but he can't lift his foot off. He has to do that with his hands, and he got stuck."

"And you're driving with him to Florida like that?" I asked.

Well, I'm not sure I remember exactly which year that was, but yes they drove, and yes they made it without injury or further incident.

This year, 2012, I received the call that my Dad received a speeding ticket in North

Carolina. Heaven help the poor state trooper who walked up to the car window. You see, Auntie Mary is a semi-celebrity in Bristol because she worked for the Chief of Police for over twenty years and is quite familiar with the types of issues that befall a small suburban town of 40,000 or so that pass before the Chief's desk. My Mom, a distinctive inquisitor in her own right, shouldered up with Auntie Mary, and they began their dialog, more like an interrogation, of the trooper. Keep in mind that all three—my Mom, Dad, and Auntie Mary—are in their 80s.

So, as soon as the trooper made his prototypical request for license, insurance, and registration and asked the obligatory question of "Do you know how fast you were going? 86 miles per hour by the way," he added, before anyone can respond Auntie Mary launched into a full-blown Perry Mason. She asked in rapid fire: "When is the last time you had your radar gun calibrated? When did you last change the battery? What other objects were in your radar sight line? How much experience do you have with a radar gun? When did you last update your training certificate on radar?"

The trooper politely held up his hand, cut her off, and stated that he was not going to try the case here on the side of the road, but Mr. McCain would be free to hire a lawyer and present these questions in court.

At this point, my Mom chimed in: "You can't possibly give him a ticket, officer, because it's not his fault. You see, he has a bad leg and it gets stuck on the accelerator and he can't take it off. Besides, he's on so much medication that he's woozy and light-headed. You can't possibly hold that against him."

I don't know if my Dad at this point was laughing, crying, trying to swat them both away with a wave of his massive hand, or what. All I know is that the trooper did something I don't think I would have done after hearing about my Dad's leg and medication in that he simply issued the speeding ticket and bid them goodbye to continue to make their way south, leg, medication, and all. I'll bet he was secretly hoping that some other trooper would pull them over and have to endure what he had just gone through.

Eventually, the three of them—my Mom, Dad, and Auntie Mary—arrived as planned in Hallandale. They never take more than three days to make the drive, stopping at a small circle of pre-ordained roadside motels, stopping by 6 p.m. or so and starting on the road no later than 7 a.m.

Every year when they arrive, they look a little worn. I suppose it's a combination of age, brutal New England winters, the hard road pace they set for themselves, and being on the declining side of health. This year was no different. My Dad especially looked weak, off balance, and ashen in color. Sometimes, through unfortunate experience, one begins to develop a sense of the healing powers of the human body and spirit, despite having no medical degree or training. Such is the lens with which I viewed my Dad upon his arrival. When I asked my Mom and my brother Tim, they both said something to the effect of "He's been bad like this before, but he'll recover."

When I asked my Aunt and my cousins (almost all of whom have had medical-related careers), they were less optimistic and more concerned. I was definitely in their camp but cautiously, unrealistically, optimistic.

Dad arrived using a cane to walk around and of course walls, pieces of furniture, my shoulder, and other objects to supplement his support. That was similar to prior years. Usually, by the second or so week of Florida sunshine and warmth, he would have color and energy. But not this year; that didn't happen; he didn't improve. He fought hard but gradually declined. He walked less and less; more than ten or fifteen steps was an effort.

My Dad slept with an oxygen mask, again resisting until it was long overdue and mandatory, but he always felt embarrassed letting people know, or, heaven forbid, wearing oxygen in public.

Not this year. In order to function, he started using portable oxygen during the day. He began to stop cursing at the suggestion that he use a wheelchair to get around some. Those were two huge signs for me.

As the Florida time passed, he twice found himself in the local hospital: once for fluid in the lungs, and once for a near-fatal diabetic coma.

By Easter Sunday, at the suggestion of my wife, Margarita, he was in a wheelchair full time. He was also on full-time oxygen. His appetite was nearly non-existent, which, for a McCain, is unthinkable. He lost nearly 35 pounds from January to April. Despite his deterioration, we had a great Easter celebration of family. We started discussing the concept of my driving the three of them back to Connecticut instead of Dad driving. It really wasn't much of a discussion; really more of a sad realization.

That night around 8 p.m., shortly after the three arrived back in Hallandale, I received a call from my Mom that Dad's blood sugar was way too low and that emergency was on its way. It had been low while they were at our house for Easter, but it steadied and rose enough to go to Hallandale. Now, however, it was alarmingly and shockingly low. He fell, passed out, was revived, and they called emergency. God bless my cousin Judy, who was often a primary caretaker, who was there that evening. Eventually, the hospital remedied his "sugar" issue, but the medical staff was reluctant to tinker with much else, especially the twenty-plus prescription drug buffet he took daily.

As for me, at this point, I knew what was to come. My outlook shifted from eternal hope and squeezing the last ounce out of being a little boy with a magical and heroic Dad, to a son acting as a parent trying to provide as much comfort and love as I could during a period that I knew was going to be sadly and forever too short, no matter whether it was to last one week, one month, one year, or one decade.

On April 15, 2012, with a packed and loaded car, we left Hallandale at approximately 8 a.m. "We" consisted of Mom and Auntie Mary in the back seat, my Dad in the front as the passenger, and me driving. The car was my Mom's relatively new four-door Honda Accord.

Part II. My Honor

Judy and Margarita eased us into the car. I could tell they were both as unbelieving as I that we were leaving, that we intended to get there (Connecticut), and that we would take no more than three days to do so. I vividly recall the long goodbyes, the unknowing, heartfelt gaze in their eyes, and them both slightly shaking their heads in disbelief as we shoved off. I felt as though we were suspended in a Titanic-like underwater bubble, saying goodbye to one world and entering another.

After a very short silence of no less than a quarter mile, my Mom and Auntie Mary broke the silence with their drive chatter: "Doesn't he drive so smoothly?" "He changes lanes so effortlessly." "What a great driver." All of these accolades and we had yet to travel five minutes up the road, get gas, or start our journey on I-95.

The car was meticulously packed. One overnight bag each, foldable wheelchair, portable oxygen, suitcase full of prescription drugs, walking canes, shoes, and miscellaneous in the trunk; large living room oxygen tank (the size of a college dorm room refrigerator), blankets, three days' worth of packed lunches and liquids in the back seat; maps, cell phones, and GPS devices in the back and front seats.

The first of our episodes occurred at the gas station between the Hallandale condo and I-95, which was approximately seven or eight minutes, or less than five miles, from our starting point. We needed gas. I pulled in, turned off the car, started pumping, squeegeed the windows, and got back in ready to go. I was proud of my gas pumping-window cleaning prowess. I was the model of efficiency. Inside the car however, things were not perfect. You see, I had, as anyone else would, turned off the car to pump the gas. When I did, even though it took less than three minutes, the oxygen, which was plugged into the lighter, turned off, even though the machine still made noise. My Dad was not breathing well. Why didn't they tell me? Why didn't I ask? Why didn't we plan? None of us knew these things. Regardless, lesson learned. My Dad, who needed oxygen only when he slept some three months ago, now could not go three minutes without. Thank God we had the portable oxygen. My prayer at that moment was that we had enough portable oxygen to last us for all the stops we would need to make on our three-day journey and that we could indeed actually complete our journey in the three allotted days.

I had never changed oxygen before. Why would I have? Changing oxygen for me was as foreign as the need to speak Russian or the need to know how to sail a nuclear submarine. I learned fast. I remembered a conversation and lesson my Dad had given me the year before, one of those lessons that while you are receiving it it's all you can do to pay attention because you know it will never apply to you and you'll never need to use it.

Within the next two hours, I became the best and most efficient oxygen tank changer you would ever meet. No one could possibly be better. I learned to change oxygen as though it were a matter of life and death. Because it was: my Dad's life depended on my doing and being so.

The I-95 highway entrance was about a half-mile from the gas station. We entered in relative silence after our gas station oxygen episode. Shortly thereafter, the driving accolades started again. That was our driving ice breaker. Right about then, we started discussing our driving ground rules. We would look to stop every two hours or so. We would look to break around five or six p.m., and we would stay somewhere modest. Lunch for everyone was packed and we would eat in the car or at one of the rest stops. None of this was an issue for me. I love to drive. I find it therapeutic, and I had driven from Florida to Connecticut or vice versa dozens of times, though not in at least ten years and not with my parents since 1977, some 35 years earlier. We would stop at the designated rest areas on I-95; at least, that was our plan, unless facts dictated otherwise.

Facts shortly thereafter dictated otherwise. Hallandale Beach Boulevard is exit 18 off of I-95. The exit system is simple and understandable. Each exit represents the mile marker within which it occurs. I-95 starts in Miami at mile marker 1 and ends north of Jacksonville, Florida, somewhere in the 400s. In south Georgia, it starts at exit 1 again, etc. Anyway, according to our ground rules, our target was to stop approximately 120 miles north of the Hallandale exit 18 mile marker, or, around mile marker 140. We didn't get that far. My Dad needed to stop. We had not yet seen a rest stop, nor were we much more than an hour or an hour and ten minutes into our trip. We were, however, past the busy urban sections of Broward and Palm Beach counties and had clearly entered an agricultural setting where the exits, instead of occurring every mile or two, were 10, 15, or even more miles apart.

He needed to stop; we took the next exit. I'll never forget the exit—Hobe Sound. I've lived in Florida nearly 30 years. I've heard of Hobe Sound dozens of times. Surely they had a restroom. I exited the highway. I drove east, toward civilization. Nothing. Tree farms, nothing. Tree farms and nothing. That's what we passed for the next ten minutes. Finally, I came to a spot where we could pull into a small warehouse complex, unoccupied on this Sunday morning, where my Dad could get out and relieve himself in the bushes.

We stopped. I got out and walked to his door. I opened it. He looked at me. I looked at him. I could tell he couldn't get up. I helped him stand. He was still over 350 pounds, despite his weight loss. His legs were useless and weak. More ornamental than anything else, like the legs of a newborn not yet able to stand. I stood him up and helped him to a tree. He couldn't go. He couldn't breathe. We had gone as far as the oxygen line would permit. He needed something, anything, and all I knew was that I was unable to give it to him. He leaned against the tree helplessly. He shook as he stood and leaned. He asked that I take him back to the car, which I did. I sat him down. He rested and closed his eyes as he sat in the car. I prayed to God to please let me bring this great man home. Please don't let him die on the side of the road. Please God, bless him; take him into your arms and your great light. Let me bring him home.

We continued our journey. We made our way back to I-95 and mercifully, while Hobe Sound disappeared in the background at exit 96, there was a real honest-to-goodness rest stop at mile marker 106. We stopped. We now had the workings of a plan. We parked with the car still running. I popped the trunk and dug out the portable oxygen tank. I unzipped the carrying case, turned the release valve counter clockwise as far as I could with the custom wrench attached to the tank with a chain, unfurled the plastic breathing tube, set the oxygen regulator valve to the appropriate flow, and brought it to my Dad. I placed the tubing around his ears and the nose stem in his nostrils at the same time I removed the larger, car-based oxygen unit tube from his nose. I placed the portable tank in his lap as I quickly made my way around the car, turned the ignition off, unplugged the large unit from the lighter and turned it off. "Need to save that oxygen tank battery," one of them said, though at this moment, while I can't remember whether my Mom or Aunt said that, the comment was certainly prophetic. After turning the car and large oxygen unit off, I returned to the trunk. Out came the portable wheelchair. I spread the seat, locked it in place, and sped to his door. I needed to place the chair just so: close enough to maneuver him in, not so close as to prevent me from lifting him into it. He out stretched his arms and placed them around my neck. I bear-hugged him and placed my arms under his armpits all the way—as close as we could get—until our chest and bellies were touching. I got into a squat position and stood, lifting him and trying not to fall over at the same time. From there we shuffled around in a half circle until he was lined up to sit down and not miss the chair. Since his legs had no strength, we repeated our movement with me squatting down instead of up until he was safely in the chair. Next, I reached into the car for the portable oxygen tank and hung it off of the back of the wheelchair. We would become quite skilled at our dance and rarely tangled the oxygen tube, or, heaven forbid, pulled it from his nose.

Part II. My Honor

Next, I backed him away from the car door, closed and locked the door and trunk, and began pushing or pulling him to the men's room. You see, in our packing haste, we never thought of the foot rests for the portable wheelchair. So, while my Dad was able to ride in the chair, with regard to his legs his choices were as follows: he could either be pushed from behind and face forward while holding his feet in the air or, if too tired, I would pull him and he could let his feet drag or bounce along the pavement on his heels. Both had pluses and minuses, but that's what we had. It became our running commentary, with either humor or frustration, depending on his mood and tolerance level at the moment.

Once in the chair, we made our way to the men's room. I'm not sure what I expected but it surely wasn't what happened. I've spent little time in a wheelchair and the small amount of time I have done so was because of a sports injury, temporary infirmary, etc. It was never because I was unable to move, like my Dad, like now.

We entered the restroom—me awkwardly pushing and pulling the chair while simultaneously opening the door, in this case double doors, one pair of doors was set several feet behind the other for privacy, which added to the awkwardness of entering—and looked around. We went straight to the handicapped stall. I still was unsure what to expect or what to do. I found out soon enough.

We entered the stall. I muscled the chair around until the angles made sense. From there we repeated our car dance routine. I bear-hugged my Dad. He placed his arms around my neck. I stood him up. I rolled his pants down and then bear-hugged and sat him down on the toilet. I confirmed that his oxygen was in place and exited the stall.

When it was time for me to return, he rapped his cane on the floor. Upon entry, we did the bear-hug, stood up, cleaned whatever needed cleaning, pulled his pants up, bear-hugged to sit back in the wheelchair, and exited the stall. We wheeled up to the sink and I washed his hands with soap and warm water and dried them, just like he used to do for me. We exited the restroom with a smile. We took in the sunshine for a minute or two and then made our way to the car. I opened the door, opened the trunk, positioned the wheelchair just so, and we went through our bear-hug up, bear-hug down-switch out the oxygen-dance, packed the wheelchair into the trunk, confirmed with my Mom and Auntie Mary that they were okay, and were on our way. Each stop then, assuming no complications, would take about 45 minutes. After the mile marker 106 stop, I was convinced it would take at least a week to get Dad home. I prayed that God would let him make it.

After mile marker 106, we stopped a mere 25 minutes later at marker 133. We danced, bear-hugged, rode in the chair, visited the men's room, and hugged, road, and danced some more. At this pace, I changed my mind. I was thinking it might take the month of April to get to Connecticut. My selfish and unrealistic goal, back in the world where the rest of us lived, was to be in Fort Lauderdale by Friday, April 20, to make it to the high school regional track and field championships to watch Danny compete. I was certain I would be hearing about the meet from the road. While it was not yet noon on Sunday the 15th, the 20th seemed a lifetime away.

Once back in the car, Dad fell asleep. We passed the stops at mile markers 168, 189, and 209 as he slept. He woke right before the rest stop at marker 225 and we stopped to perform our dance. We drove the remainder of the day, stopping when he was awake at every rest area we passed, driving steadily past others as he drifted in and out of sleep.

At 1:30 or so, my Mom asked if we were ready for lunch.

"Sure," I replied nonchalantly even though I was starving.

She gave me a cookie and half of a peanut butter sandwich with two mismatched pieces of bread. I realized her idea of a packed lunch and mine were vastly different. When we next stopped for gas, I bought some protein bars and tucked them into my knapsack. I bought water too. None of them drink much of it, preferring diet sodas and juices instead. I'm used to drinking at least a gallon a day.

"We don't really eat a big lunch on the road," she said.

"No matter," I replied, "I'll adapt. Besides, I have protein bars now. I can go days of eating nothing else if necessary."

"What's a protein bar?" she asked. I laughed and offered her one.

Sometime shortly after the five o'clock hour the debate began as to where and when we would stop for the day. I suggested that I was ready to drive until nine or ten or even later if necessary. They politely declined and suggested we stop soon.

We were somewhere in south Georgia, having recently crossed the Florida state line. We pulled off the highway at the state line welcome center and did our dance routine. Mom and Auntie Mary gathered brochures with coupons to get the best hotel rates possible. Our target: no more than $44.95 per night. We pulled into the parking lot of the first potential motel. Three stories, semi-trailer trucks in the parking lot, rusted stairwells, no elevators, visible signs of attempted forced entry on many of the first-floor room doors, and the busy highway noise. Mom and Auntie Mary went in to negotiate. Dad suddenly was awake and alert for the first time that day. I realized how much I adored his company and we started discussing our day, my sons, colleges, the holidays, and life in general. After five or ten minutes or so, Mom and Auntie Mary returned with several room keys, stating that they needed to check out the rooms because they weren't all together, one on the first floor and two on the second.

At that moment, one of the classic verbal arguments broke out as to why we needed this type versus that type of room; let's stay, let's go; why are we deciding this by committee, etc. After a few minutes, Dad sent them away and declared we would try another motel. He complained while they were gone that this committee process was ridiculous and that we should plan better. I didn't mind his frustrations. He was spirited and alert. I smiled and he laughed.

We moved down the road and found an acceptable $44.95 per night accommodation. After inspections and haggling, we moved into our rooms. Unloading and getting into the room took the same 45 minutes that was required for our rest area stops. Unfortunately, it was now pushing seven o'clock and we needed dinner. So, we ambled back into the car and looked for a restaurant. After several debates, rejections, menu inspections and dead ends, we stopped at a non-franchised Chinese buffet-type of restaurant. We had relatively little, virtually nothing, to eat all day. I was really hungry, and I assumed they were too.

Dad ordered soup, Mom and Auntie Mary pepper steak, rice and chicken. I ordered broccoli and chicken. The food came to the table. I ate the most: three bites. On a good day, the food was best described as horrible, inedible, and disgusting. Thank God this was a good day. We dutifully paid and left, returning to the hotel. I ate three protein bars and a bottle of water from the vending machine.

We nestled into our rooms, chatted away for an hour or two, and eventually slept. Well, at least I did. I think Auntie Mary did too. My Mom and Dad were awake much of the night doing what they needed to do. Fortunately, they had a handicapped room so the bathroom and shower were readily accessible.

We agreed to meet at 6:45 for breakfast in the lobby. The motel had powdered scrambled eggs, mushy oatmeal, prepackaged muffins, too-old brown speckled bananas, and old apples. I ate like a king at his daughter's wedding banquet and washed it down with all the stale black coffee I could muster. I knew from yesterday that lunch was not to be.

We drove through the day, stopping and starting, doing our dance, and not eating, just like the day before. Sometime during mid-day, late morning if I recall, the portable oxygen tank ran out—empty. After an extremely difficult rest area dance, where Dad could barely breathe, we discovered our ignorance. Fortunately, we had a second filled tank and we were now more than halfway home. Besides, we thought, we have the large oxygen machine in the car, which we plugged into the regular wall socket in our motel room nightly. We changed out the portable oxygen tank and continued our journey.

Late that travel day, sometime in the three or four o'clock hour, disaster struck. The large oxygen machine stopped working. We pulled off of the highway into a gas station. We sought repairs, bathrooms, and protein bars.

We took turns using the single bathroom; there was a line. I vividly recall feeling no shame at almost knocking over a small boy as he tried to enter the bathroom door I had forgotten to lock while I was cleaning Dad. His mother looked at me in shock. The boy pounded on the door, his mother asking politely but sternly to let him in. A few moments later, I emerged with my Dad, in the chair, with his oxygen clanking and banging against the small doorway and she backed away. It was her turn to feel shame.

I bought more protein bars. I wheeled Dad up and down the aisles where he *oohed* and *aahed* at the many old-fashioned candies that he could no longer eat. We assembled at the car. I played with the large oxygen machine, read the manual, pushed buttons, plugged, unplugged, and prayed, but could not get it to work. We called Judy, who was largely responsible for packing the trunk. I had silently thanked her earlier because she had packed the spare portable oxygen tank. I was loudly and profusely thanking her now as she told me she had packed a spare battery for the large oxygen tank. I knew it was an impossibility to get to Connecticut with the remaining portable oxygen. I promptly changed the battery but nothing happened. I slowly and confidently removed the battery and put it back in but still nothing happened. I suddenly fell into that mental haze one has when you wonder if you locked the front door of your house as you are pulling out of the driveway. I questioned myself as to whether I had actually changed the battery. I changed the battery out again, now certain that I had tried both, but neither worked. Decision time. We decided to cut our travel day short and get to a hotel so we could charge the large oxygen machine battery in a wall socket instead of the car lighter socket. We would use portable oxygen as we drove. While driving, my Mom had a series of frustrating calls with Medicare, the oxygen machine company, a hospital in Florida, etc. None were helpful. Suggestions for help varied from driving several hundred miles out of our way, to calling the manufacturer, to calling back during business hours. We kept driving, looking for a hotel with a hospital nearby.

Also during that day, Dad started making motions with his hands. At first, I thought he was sleeping and dreaming. Later, I found out that he had his eyes closed and was hallucinating. At first, his hallucinations were harmless. He would place his hands on his lap and turn them over on top of each other back and forth, as though he was making a snowball or patting a towel dry. Then he would hold an imaginary object in his left hand, and make a sewing motion with his right. He'd pull a stitch through the object in his left hand and pull it tight with his right, bringing his right hand approximately chest- or ear-high across his body. After repeating this process five or six times, he would pat the object in his left hand several times and either place it in his imaginary left pants pocket or tuck it into his imaginary belt just over his left hip. After this scene had played out several times and after I realized he wasn't sleeping but merely had his eyes closed, I asked him what it was he was doing.

"Are we there yet?" he asked.

"Um, almost," I said, confused, because he must realize we were still days away from Connecticut. "Where is it that we are going again?"

"To the lake," he said. "Going fishing."

"Are you tying flies and getting your hooks ready?" I asked.

He nodded his head *yes* and continued. Dad tied a lot of hooks that day.

We eventually made it to our hotel for the evening. Dad was alert. We went through our dance and made our way to our respective rooms. Task one was to repair the oxygen machine. Dad was alert and lucid for the first time that day. He had that machine running in less than five minutes. He showed me a reset button and I memorized its location for future reference if needed. Dad could fix anything, anytime, anywhere. He was a gifted mechanic and unbelievably resourceful.

We readied ourselves for dinner. We chose an American buffet-style restaurant in the building next door. The restaurant was about fifty feet away. We drove. There was no curb cut to push the wheelchair. All of us needed food; even Dad ate that night. He managed about three tablespoons of mashed potatoes and gravy, a bite of bread, and a sliced beet. He drank a cup of water and one of apple juice.

Later that evening in the motel room, I was moving furniture in Mom and Dad's room to accommodate middle-of-the-night trips to the bathroom. I moved chairs, tables, luggage racks, and the desk, moved them back, and moved them again. Because of

Dad's condition, it was easier and more comfortable for him to sleep sitting up than lying down. As I was lifting his legs to place them on a hassock that I fashioned out of two upside down garbage cans and a luggage rack, I was startled because his legs were soaking wet. You see, during the entire trip, his legs were wrapped in ace bandages. I learned at that moment that his legs were wrapped because he had open diabetic wounds that were constantly oozing. Mom continuously wrapped and changed the bandages on Dad's legs, but the oozing was outpacing her efforts. My hands were wet and his legs were soaked. I considered it the least of our worries. We settled in, chatted until it was time to go to sleep, agreed to meet at 6:30 for breakfast, and went to our rooms to sleep.

Around three o'clock in the morning, there were sirens and flashing red lights outside my door. I prayed. I found my glasses, grabbed a shirt, and opened my door to the chilly, early morning air. I met Auntie Mary doing the same. We confirmed that, while not a false alarm, it was not my Dad's alarm. He was fine. We went back to sleep.

Breakfast was in another building near the lobby. We all agreed that I would shuttle food to the room for each of them to save time and stress. Breakfast choices were prepackaged honey buns and donuts, bananas, and Cheerios or Fruit Loops. I brought some of each. To drink, the choices were coffee, orange juice, and apple juice. I made a second trip and brought a tray of coffee and apple juice. Dad likes coffee but was not able to drink it for at least twenty years or so, so, I brought the apple juice for him. Mom and Auntie Mary like coffee with cream and Sweet'N Low. I set the trays of pastries and drinks on the table in their room and left to get coffee and Cheerios for me.

I returned to a ruckus—a little yelling, a little cursing, and a great story. Somehow, Mom had mistaken Dad's apple juice for tea. She dutifully filled it with cream and Sweet'N Low. Dad, apparently not paying strict attention, took a big gulp, promptly spit it out, and sprayed it all over the room.

The accusations flew. We eventually laughed after going through a few different versions of "How could you?" and I brought fresh apple juice.

We hit the road that morning somewhere in Virginia. It was Tuesday, April 17th. The day started like the one before it. We were comfortably rich with oxygen and within striking distance of our final destination. Dad drifted in and out of sleep and started tying fly knots again. We maneuvered through morning rush hour, guessed at the traffic infractions people were pulled over for, and cheered when we found the multi-passenger express lane. We endured the construction detour, which routed us into more bumper-to-bumper traffic through downtown Washington, D.C., and pointed out the historic monuments to each other. Dad kept tying fly knots. However, at one point while semi-waking from a nap, he suddenly and violently reached for and attempted to yank open the passenger door while I was driving. I was startled; fortunately, the doors were locked.

Part II. My Honor

Thirty or forty minutes passed and he tried again. This time, however, instead of one quick failed attempt, he repeatedly tried to open his door several times in succession. It seemed as though this lasted for half an hour but I'm sure it was only fifteen or twenty seconds. I held down the driver's side master lock with intense focus as I drove, unable to pull over, and prayed yet again, this time, that the master lock would override his attempts to open the door. The intensity of the moment eventually faded and he drifted back to sleep.

We stopped for the first time that day in northern Virginia. The weather was cool, crisp, and overcast. I remember us laughing and cursing the architect and whatever government planning board had designed and approved the rest stop. There was a handicap ramp from the parking lot to the restrooms. However, it appeared to be at least a quarter-mile long, was steeply inclined uphill, and consisted of sharp and numerous hairpin twists and turns. After our wheelchair-oxygen dance, it took at least ten minutes to scale the hill. We had to stop several times so Dad could rest from being pushed. I was more concerned about the trip down the hill; I could only imagine a runaway wheelchair. I eventually discovered that my standing on the downhill side of the wheelchair and walking backwards provided the most safety for all involved.

We continued driving and Dad drifted in and out of sleep. The road, terrain, cities and sights grew more familiar as we proceeded northward. Sometime later mid-morning, Dad began straining in his seat. He started mumbling, softly at first and then louder.

"Hurry up," he said. "I can't hold it much longer. My legs, hurry!"

"What's the matter?" I asked. "Are you okay? Do we need to find a bathroom?"

"No, no, no," he said. "My legs. I can't hold them up much longer. Hurry!"

"What do you mean?" I asked. "What's the matter with your legs? Why do you need to hold them up?"

"The road!" he exclaimed, almost shouting. "If I relax and put them down, they'll break against the road. My legs will break!"

Reality. Cold, ice water to the face. Panic. Think of something, something now, fast, immediately. Dad was full-out hallucinating.

I drew a deep breath, just like he taught me to do so many times when trouble is present. I drew the deepest of breaths and placed my hand on his now frail shoulder to soothe him, and said as gently as possible, "It's okay, Dad, you can put your legs down. They won't hit the road. We're in a strong new car. The floor is strong and will protect you. I promise. See?" I said, as I stomped my feet on the floor, making as much thumping noise as I could. "See?" I said, as I placed his hand on my knee and stomped again. Thankfully and mercifully, this soothed him and he dozed back to sleep. I shed a tear, one of many on that trip, but the first in his presence, wiped my cheek with my sleeve and kept driving. Right about then, Mom and Auntie Mary, still and always present in the back seat, asked what we were talking about up there. I lied and said, "Oh, nothing much," and I told them I would tell them more later. We continued on.

We resumed car chatter, discussed which bridges to take, and made our rest stops. We stopped in New Jersey and visited the restroom. Dad was alert and kept apologizing for how embarrassing this must be for me. "Happy to do it," I said. "Best day of my life." He smiled, shook his head back and forth and thanked me. We ordered ice cream at the rest stop and he had a few spoonfuls. We resumed driving. Mom and I had a great and spirited debate regarding New Jersey Turnpike exit 19 A and how roads and exit numbers change over the years, and we discussed the concept of old maps becoming outdated as a result. It was a great distraction for me, letting me fall into the more analytical type of discussion that I am used to and comfortable with.

We crossed the border to New York and all of us picked up with excitement just a little bit because we were that much closer to home. We shared stories of long ago family trips and travels down familiar roads, each exit along the I-95 New York-Connecticut corridor seemingly having its own story and involving various thoughts and memories. We grew more conversant and discussed the current generation of college students, how lucky we were, how proud we were of them, and relaxed just a little. Dad mostly slept.

We finally reached Connecticut and stopped for an overdue break. As we were exiting the restroom, Dad put his foot down and the wheelchair stopped. "Don't take me home," he said. "I don't want to go home. I can't go home. I want you to take me straight to Bristol Hospital. Mom can't take care of me like this. I need to go straight to the hospital."

I stared at him, blinked hard, and assured him that I would do exactly that. I would take him straight to Bristol Hospital. He was clear, alert, and resolute, as was I. I would absolutely honor this request. In fact, I had wanted to do exactly that—take him straight to the hospital, that is—and was just waiting for the right time to bring it up. Once and yet again, he made my life easier.

As we approached the car, I declared, though politely, that we were, instead of going home, proceeding directly to Bristol Hospital at Dad's request, my agreement, and more importantly, my promise to him. I'm sure there was a little bit of discussion on the topic but I didn't care or notice. I was on a mission to honor his request.

We arrived at the hospital about an hour-and-a-half later, sometime around four o'clock in the afternoon. We were checked in in less than ten minutes. I was thankful for the efficiency. Bristol is still a small town and everybody knows each other, which is just one of its many charms.

While we were in the triage unit and the nurse was "taking Dad's vitals"—blood pressure, pulse, and asking questions such as "Why are you here?"—I softly laughed because Dad was pulling his typical "I'm okay," and "Don't know what all the fuss is about," routine, even though we all knew this was the only place for him to be. He was admitted promptly. The nurse asked Mom and me to step back into the waiting room while they cleaned Dad up, placed IVs, catheters, and what not, and assigned him to a room.

We were permitted to rejoin Dad about twenty minutes later. He looked clean and peaceful and was relaxing on his gurney. We interrupted his peace with family, laughter, and a crowd: Mom, Auntie Mary, my cousin Karen, my cousin Betsy, me, various nurses, and others joined. We shared photos from our phones, stories, and enjoyed each other's company. I played Notre Dame fight songs for him from my phone until he begged me to stop, half laughing and half crying. We all laughed some more.

Sometime after seven o'clock, we were told we all had to leave and that Dad needed to have tests run, get some sleep, and have some quiet time. The male nurse and I helped Dad from his gurney to a wheelchair. When it was time to go, I blindly refused to admit to myself what I already knew: this could easily be our last earthly goodbye. We looked at each other. We hugged, we kissed, I shook his mighty hand, and we did it again. I reminded him, more realistically deluding myself, that I would see him in thirty days or so when I would return to Bristol in late May with Margarita, Danny, and Johnny to celebrate graduation, and told him that I loved him. We hugged and embraced again, he thanked me, told me he loved me too, and we parted. I looked back after a few steps; he nodded, smiled and waved. I dashed back in. We hugged one more time, and I left.

I took Mom and Auntie Mary to the grocery store, since they were just returning home in mid-April after having left in January. We picked up a few items, I dropped Auntie Mary off at her house, and Mom and I went home. It was quiet, awkward, and we were both a little lost. I emptied the car, taking pleasure in such a routine and distracting chore, and helped her set up—plugging in lamps, televisions, computers, and the like. We wandered through the house together restlessly. It was now near nine o'clock and I was to sleep at the Hartford airport hotel that night in order to catch a six-thirty morning flight to Miami. Karen came over; we drank a bottle of wine and nibbled on crackers and cheese. Mom and I said our goodbyes, each feeling a little sorry for the other, promised to speak to each other often and daily, and Karen and I made our way to the airport a little before midnight. I checked in, set the alarm for four-thirty and called Margarita. She soothed me to sleep and I awoke to the alarm.

Chapter 18: A Too-Short Return Trip to Miami

It was Wednesday morning, April 18, 2012. I rolled out of my hotel bed at 4:30 and into the airport through the connecting corridor. I boarded my flight, numbly, and fell asleep. Upon arriving home, I loved my family. I had missed them with all my heart and I showed them and told them so. We caught up from the days missed together; I told them the story of "The Drive"; and we prepared for a nice dinner, restful sleep, and a track meet. The next day Danny had a Florida Regional track meet and he qualified for the state finals the following week. We also received medical news on my Dad. He was battling congestive heart failure due to a buildup of fluid and pressure around his heart. This explained his hallucinations, as the combination of the pressures of the fluid around his heart and the need for oxygen deprived him of lucid thought, stripped him of his appetite, and prevented him from comfortably lying down, among many other discomforts.

On Friday we had a scare. Mom was called to the hospital but Dad recovered. He did well on Saturday. On Sunday morning, April 22, 2012, his heart stopped, and we lost him at 4:28.

Mom called and Margarita answered. We all knew. I was handed the phone and Mom told me. I held my composure for a long time, maybe as long as two or three seconds. Then I cried for a long, long time. I still cry today and have cried countless times writing these passages.

Margarita, Johnny, Danny and I flew up to Connecticut on Monday the 23rd, my parents' wedding anniversary. We drove straight from the airport to my Mom's house, no longer my parents' house, arriving early- to mid-afternoon. Mom greeted and comforted us. I know she appreciated our being there. I also believe she took comfort in providing comfort to us, having likely shed her tears and grieved many years earlier, since Dad had been so medically challenged for so long.

We picked at food and told stories. The table was pre-set. I remember, plateful of food in hand, freezing in place as I approached the table. My boyhood chair and regular place at the table was occupied. My Dad's chair, the head of the table, was empty. Auntie Mary saw my panic. She gently walked over to my Dad's chair, pulled it out, and said, "You sit here now, David," and walked away. Chills ran through my body. My arms filled with goosebumps. I looked at the scene around me, swallowed hard at the lump in my throat, and proceeded to sit. I looked into and saw the future, which was the present. I had grown into my father's chair, the head of the table. We continued as though he had never left. We ate and talked and eventually made our way back to the hotel to change and relax for ten minutes.

That evening we attended my Dad's wake. Judy had collected a ton of pictures and had done a remarkable job both in displaying them and in the breadth of beautiful memories she had recaptured.

I looked at my Dad, embalmed and at rest, and remember thinking to myself that that wasn't him. He had already left, and Dad and I had already said our goodbyes. His body was simply on display for others to visit and take their turns at grieving and saying goodbye. We had been given the privilege, the honor, and the gift, of saying goodbye and basking in each other's presence during The Drive. A gift of over 60 hours of nonstop time together that few sons receive to say goodbye to and love their fathers in such complete and uninterrupted fashion. For that, I am truly and forever grateful.

Shortly thereafter, people started to arrive. Old and young, they came to pay their respects and say goodbye. My Mom, brother Tim and his wife Debi, Margarita and I formed a line and shook hands, embraced, and shared short pleasant exchanges with what seemed like thousands of people. This went on for a few hours. I heard many,

many kind words about my Dad that night. He made a lasting impression on so many and different people. I was both proud of and happy for him.

After the wake, family and friends gathered at Betsy's house. We shared more food, wine, and stories. It was a quiet and gentle celebration. The next morning, we were back at the funeral home. There was a beautiful military gun salute, accompanied by the presentation of an American flag, the spent bullet shells from the salute, and, most impactfully, my cousin Scott in full Navy dress uniform. This was the only time during the entire whirlwind of several days of activities when my Mom cried. The ceremony, though brief, was moving and brought forth a flood of emotions.

From the funeral home and Mass, we went to Nuchie's restaurant for more family, food, and celebration. Nearly all of my cousins, aunts, and uncles were there. I hadn't seen many of them in years—too many years. I was both elated at rekindling our love and admiration for each other and, at the same time, sad and disappointed with myself that so many years had passed, so many lives had passed, with far too many absences and missed opportunities to get together. I recall almost clinging to my Uncle Tom, the last surviving McCain of his generation, because he reminded me of my Dad so much. It was both painful and soothing talking to and being with him. His voice, his looks, his stature, his cadence, even his scent. I couldn't drink him in quickly or voluminously enough.

My loyal, trusted, and best friends showed as well over that weekend. John, Jeff, Peter, and Tim. I remember crying at one of our last high school graduation parties some 30 years earlier (back when showing emotion, let alone crying, was definitely "un-cool"), telling them that we might never see each other or be as close again as we went our separate ways off to college. Fortunately, while the years and miles have separated us, we seem to find each other when we need each other most. I wish that type and strength of friendship upon everyone, especially my two sons.

Part II. My Honor

The next day, Thursday, April 26th, we flew home—Margarita, Johnny, Danny, and me. Johnny returned to his life in Las Vegas and on Friday the 27th, Margarita, Danny, and I drove from Miami to Jacksonville, about eight hours and 400 miles, to attend the high school state track and field championship meet where Danny was competing in the discus.

On Saturday morning, Danny threw. He hit his best mark ever, setting a personal and school best at 140' 10", ended up medaling, and placed fifth in the state. After a short celebration on Saturday afternoon, we hopped back into the car and drive over 200 miles to Orlando so Danny could attend "Senior Night," one of his last high school activities, at Universal Studios and theme park. We arrived shortly after 10 o'clock and helped Danny catch up to his classmates. Margarita and I ate a late dinner, followed by coffee, and at approximately 11:30 p.m., drove to Miami. Arriving just after 2:45 a.m. on Sunday the 29th, we waited for Danny to arrive by bus with the rest of his classmates. Exhausted, we picked him up at his school sometime around 6 that morning.

Around 11 a.m. or so later that morning, I decided I needed a good workout to de-stress from the previous two weeks' activities.

I put on my workout clothes, strolled into the garage, opened the door, and backed the car out into the driveway so I could have full use of the garage space. As I was getting out of the car, having backed it into the driveway, a mere 20-foot drive, my back went out. I have degenerative discs and every once in a while there is severe, debilitating pain as bone rubs on bone. I had been through this before and it can last anywhere from several hours to a few days of barely being able to move. I painfully crumpled slow motion-like onto the driveway. Margarita and Danny were fast asleep after having pulled an all-nighter and no one was around. After the passage of some time, how much I cannot say because I had no watch or phone, I had made quite a sweat puddle on the driveway from lying in the hot sun, which was scorching both the black tar and me. I managed to crawl onto and into the cool, shaded concrete floor of the garage. There, I was able to roll over and lie on my back, close my eyes, and fall asleep briefly as tears of sorrow and pain, both spiritual and physical, ran down the sides of my face and into my ears. After what was likely an hour, I managed to crawl on my hands and knees, ever so gingerly and slowly, three or four inches at a time, painfully resting in between each movement, into the family room and onto the couch. I even managed to turn on the TV.

Sometime around two or three o'clock in the afternoon, Margarita woke and found me on the couch watching a movie. I remember her playfully teasing me saying, "Ah, it must be nice to do nothing, lie on the couch, and watch a movie." When I told her I couldn't move and relayed my story we briefly laughed and asked each other, "What next?!"

I suggested she go to the garage, close the car door, bring it back into the garage, and close the garage door as well.

From there, I ended up flat on my back and in bed, but for crawling on my hands and knees to go to the bathroom or bathe, for over ten days. I guess the stress of the previous two weeks had finally caught up with me.

All the while though, stuck on my back, I thought of The Drive and how lucky and blessed I was to have spent that time with my Dad. A time that so few of us, in today's day and age, filled with commitments, activities, too-long work weeks, and the daily clutter of life, could ever have managed. It reminded me of a conversation I had with a work friend at the height of our busiest special project 80-hour corporate work weeks, when attending a family event, if even for 45 minutes, was a major accomplishment and potential career suicide. I was asked how I "found the time" to take a family vacation. Though I didn't realize it then, my response, some ten years earlier, was perhaps prophetic, but more importantly, telling of the character my Dad had instilled in me. You don't "find the time," I said, "you take the time. You snatch and defend it with all your might and guard it voraciously, because at the end of the day, family, not work, is all that matters. Nothing we do here is more important than our families."

I Love You Dad

Part III: Warm Recollections

Chapter 19: Memories

I couldn't possibly recount the unending and seemingly infinite memories I have surrounding my Dad. Nor could I do justice to trying to fill in the gaps of what happened in his life from the time he was drafted in 1955 to the winter and spring of 2012, his last. I can, however, share with you a few things that he shared with me.

I know, for instance, that despite his hoping he would not be drafted—he was, after all, only a few months away from being exempt at the age of 25—that he ultimately very much enjoyed and was patriotically proud of most of his military time. Other than one horrible 20-day passage on a troop ship from Seattle to Japan, where sea sickness was a matter of degree, not of whether you had it or not, he raved about his time in Japan. Dad ended up in military intelligence and was assigned to live with a post-World War II Japanese family and observe their culture and customs. I remember Dad's telling and retelling with fondness the daily routine of the family elder, who would spend nearly his entire day sitting under a cherry blossom tree in the family garden meditating and drinking tea. I remember Dad being elated that he was eventually invited to spend a series of days meditating with the family elder.

Another Japanese story Dad loved to tell was how he had ridden his American-made motor scooter from the U.S. Army base into the hills and mountains of the Japanese countryside and that one day, several hours from base, he had a mechanical breakdown. After walking the scooter for an hour or so, he ran into an older gentleman walking through a country village. While they were unable to speak to each other because of the language barrier, Dad was able to communicate the mechanical issue and, astonishingly, as Dad always told it, the man produced the needed bolt that fit perfectly, matching threads and all. Dad loved to share how amazing he thought it was that two countries recently at war, one halfway around the world from the other, had matching bolt thread designs. "A true miracle of mechanics," he would call it.

Dad also loved to talk about the "Rice Bowl": the first, last, and only college football all-star game played in Japan as he told it, although I think there have been others. It wasn't the game itself that mesmerized him; rather, it was what the game represented to him personally. Apparently, one of the senior Army officers who was in charge of one of the teams had heard of Dad's football prowess and recruited Dad to be an assistant coach. That coaching duty relieved Dad of what would have been some very difficult and dangerous missions. Also, he was exposed to some of the most talented football All-Americans of that era. It wasn't until years later, while writing this book together actually, that Dad shared with me the game program and some relevant articles. One article in particular was written about one of the all-star players who was attending Brown University, interrupted by his military service obligations of course, and how Brown so impressed Dad at the time. Dad shared with me then that that was one of the reasons why he was so proud that I had attended Brown, having formed an early favorable opinion of it.

As a boy, I always thought that Dad drew the easier "parent straw" as it related to my brother and me. Dad obviously worked at and earned the family living, but at home he was mostly in charge of silliness and fun. My Mom only used him as the last resort bad cop, usually saying something like "Don't make me tell your father" whenever we were misbehaving. When Dad did discipline us, he would make us extend one arm, with the palm facing upward. He would take hold of our outstretched hands with his massive pipe-sized fingers and use

two of them—the index and the middle—
and slap us on the wrist. After he did this,
he would usually wink, put his index finger
to his lips making the "shushing" sign, and
tell us "not to do it again," whatever the
offensive "it" of the moment had been. We
would all giggle or laugh and go on about
our day. Both he and we would then tell
Mom later on that he really "gave it to us"
and that we wouldn't ever do "it" again,
having learned our lesson.

Dad also liked to sing silly songs to us. I'm
sure he made up most of the lyrics as they
were tumbling out of his mouth. However, I
have managed to remember or find a few of
them. I even managed to pass the songs on
to my boys when they were little.

The first song was the "Foot in the Noodle
Soup" song. I tried but was unable to find
the lyrics. As memory serves, it went
something like this:

One day when I was hungry,

I did not dare to steal,

I went to David McCain's house,

I Love You Dad

And asked him for a meal.

I looked at him,

He looked at me,

He thought I was a thief,

And then he asked me in for a meal,

But oh I could not eat.

A bug was on the table,

A pig behind the door,

And David's foot in the noodle soup,

I won't go there anymore!!

While I cannot convey the musical tune to you, I'm sure you can see that among 5- to 10-year-old boys and girls this was a real knee-slapping giggler.

The next song we used to call "Daddy's Whiskers." I actually found this song on the internet and the real title is "Father's Old Grey Whiskers Song." The origin is said to be from the Boy Scouts of America, which makes sense because Dad was an Eagle Scout. We used to sing and make up endless verses to this tune. Some of the lyrics I found and remember go as follows:

Intro

I have a dear old daddy
For whom I nightly pray.
He has a set of whiskers,
They're always in the way.

Chorus

Oh, they're, always in the way
The cows eat them for hay
They hide the dirt on daddy's shirt
They're always in the way!

Verses we used to sing

We have a dear old mommy
With him she nightly sleeps.
She wakes up in the morning
Thinks she's eating shredded wheat!

Chorus

Oh, they're, always in the way

I Love You Dad

The cows eat them for hay
They hide the dirt on daddy's shirt
They're always in the way!

Verse

When Daddy goes a-swimming
No bathing suit for him.
He wraps his whiskers round his waist
And then he jumps right in!

Chorus

Oh, they're always in the way
The cows eat them for hay
They hide the dirt on daddy's shirt
They're always in the way!

Verse

When daddy goes a-fishing,
No fishing pole for him.
He ties a worm right to his beard
And then he throws it in!

Chorus

Oh, they're always in the way

Part III: Warm Recollections

The cows eat them for hay

They hide the dirt on daddy's shirt

They're always in the way!

You get the point. With a good imagination and a little talent, you could go on forever, which we often did, laughing louder and longer with each silly, made-up verse.

Now, by some near miracle, Tim found an old tape recorder partially melted by the fire that took his house in the mid-1990s. Tim did not know I had included the Noodle Soup or Daddy's Whiskers songs as part of the book. However, on this tape, with a note that said "Recordings 1966-67," was a trio of singers laughing and playfully singing the Noodle Soup and Daddy's Whiskers songs. The trio? My Dad in the lead, with Tim and me joining in. My Dad would have been 35 or 36 years old at the time, while Tim and I would have been somewhere between the ages of four and six. There were even two new verses that I had not previously remembered! I hope you enjoy them. They are as follows:

I Love You Dad

Verse

When Daddy goes a-riding
In his old Ford machine,
He uses those gray whiskers
To strain the gasoline!

Chorus

Oh, they're always in the way...

Verse

When Daddy goes to war
To fight the enemy,
He'll hide behind his whiskers,
And they'll think that he's a tree!

Chorus

Oh, they're always in the way...

As we aged, Dad provided advice as we needed it or when we asked. He didn't meddle in our day-to-day issues; likely due to a combination of having his own to deal with and of his philosophy of guiding us to growth as opposed to dictating our growth. He let us fall when we needed to fall and helped us up when we needed it most. Mostly, however, he simply taught us how to be responsible, how to be humble, the difference between right and wrong, and the ability to see good in everything and everyone.

Chapter 20: Uncle Tom's recollections

When Uncle Tom and I spoke at Dad's wake celebration party, he told me, among many other things, that Dad, in his final days, raved to him about two things. First, "what a champ" I had been for undertaking "The Drive." At this point, our eyes watered as we held each other's gaze and subsequently embraced. And second, our book project. Dad had been talking to Uncle Tom throughout the writing process. I think it helped them uncover and share old memories for which they were both grateful. At this point, Uncle Tom offered, and Margarita had previously privately suggested to me, that he help review and contribute to Dad's story. So, being forever grateful and thankful to Uncle Tom, here are his memories.

Childhood

I have almost no recall of the days we lived on Osgood Avenue and I have only a few flashes of the Israel Putnam School kindergarten, where I attended for a half-year. I do remember my adult brothers laughing as they told stories of how, at times when they were responsible for me as a baby, they'd park my carriage in the shade of a convenient bush, enjoy ball games with their friends, and then push me home. (I've heard the story enough times that I've come to believe it!)

Winter, and we were among the first to live in the Murray Heights development. Everything reacted to the sub-zero temperatures, including the one-piece roll of linoleum kitchen floor tile tied to the rear of the moving van. The ropes loosened as we bounced along; the tile fell and shattered into a zillion tiny pieces, as though it was safety glass. We couldn't even clean it up.

Our new house had plaster walls, oak floors, and a partial cellar, with a living room, kitchen, three bedrooms, and a bath. When we walked in, the walls were coated with ice because of the cold, so Pop's first order of business was to get a fire going in the hot-air furnace. I guess it warmed up because I am sure I'd remember if it were cold in bed on that the first night.

At one point during World War II when I was about six or seven, Russell, David, and I were having a pillow fight in our bedroom. WHAM! I caught one on the side of the head, flew to my left and slammed into the steel bed across the room. It took several stitches to reconnect my right nostril. The silver lining to this dark cloud was the nylon stitches. At a time when women across the country could not buy nylon stockings, I had some in my nose!

Teen Years

Peter Pup was a friend to all of us and the whole family played with him, each in his own way. Russell would bring the whole family to tears of laughter with Peter Pup and a handful of stick pretzels. He'd lie on his back, holding a pretzel between his lips and invite Peter to take it. Never was the dog successful on the first try, for just as he reached for it Russell would suck the pretzel into his mouth. Peter would step back and tilt his head in wonder, only to see the pretzel reappear. Over and over the trick would replay, until Russell could no longer control his laughter, or he would let the dog win.

Houses were pretty close together in Murray Heights and neighbors were friendly. Mother never had a job outside our home, but she did take care of Stevie DeMugno, son of a young couple across the street. Stevie would stop in at our house after school and stay until his mom came home for supper.

It was always dark in the winter. Russell was very much involved in tending to Stevie and me. He told stories and roughhoused with us, but he never seemed to win the wrestling matches, even though we were two-on-one. Many times he'd send Stevie home with his coat buttoned up to the neck, but backwards. I know we thought it was fun; Mother didn't seem to mind and Mrs. DeMugno never complained.

One winter Russell decided to set up a BB gun shooting gallery in our hallway. He bought a Daisy Air Rifle, ammunition and targets, and draped bed sheets across the bedroom door at the end of the hall and around the walls on both sides. Books were used as weights on the bottom of the sheets to pull them away from the walls. BBs simply hit the sheets and rolled to the floor so we could collect and reuse them. They never hit the door or the walls.

It was about fifteen feet from the firing line to targets pinned to the sheets. Each of us got to be pretty accurate shots, and years later we all scored Expert on the U.S. Army firing ranges.

Russell was an outstanding student in the Industrial Arts department. Art Kevorkian the shop teacher was also football coach and became an inspiration for Russ in both areas. Russell made the usual tie rack and bookends as an underclassman, but later in high school he built a jewelry box as a gift for Mother. It resembled a miniature blanket chest—a little larger than a shoe box—standing on end. With its exquisite hardware and deep, rich, hand-rubbed finish, it was a treasure that stayed on her dresser for the rest of her life.

Mr. Kevorkian was so impressed with Russell's football skills that he invited him to play on New Britain's semi-professional team with him and another BHS coach, Roy Fabian. They played together for a few years and it was that connection that led to Russell's full scholarship at Moorhead State University.

One Christmas when I was about eight or nine, I had bugged my father so much about opening presents with my name on them that he gave me permission to open just one during the day of Christmas Eve. I invited a friend to join me and chose to open my largest box. My friend and I began playing with the most amazing football action game I had ever seen. Of course Mother was not at home. Russell was the first to arrive. He was surprised, agitated, and clearly disappointed with me. He calmly explained how Pop's permission was meant to give me an inch and I had taken a mile.

The package I chose to open was the gift Pop had bought for me, and he had told Russell how pleased he was with it. Russell asked me to imagine how sad Pop would be if he missed seeing the look on my face when I opened his special gift. "I think you should wrap it up again and pretend on Christmas Eve that this never happened," he said. I got the message, followed his advice, and Pop was never the wiser. He and all of us boys shared Photo Electric Football for years, playing as pairs or in teams, and I learned a lesson on the joy of giving to others.

Many years later I realized this was one of many the important parenting moments that Russell and I had shared. When I thanked him for his important role in my upbringing he simply said, "I was just practicing my fathering skills on you and Stevie."

After we got our first TV set, we spent many hours together in the living room watching baseball, football, bowling, boxing and Pop's all-time favorite, professional wrestling. We all knew the outcome was rigged, but we got pretty much involved anyway, especially Pop. We cheered the good guys and scorned the bad ones. Pop, who always sat erect on the front edge of the couch, really got into it.

He would bounce, twist, and roll when the good guy started dishing it out to the villain. We were all struck dumb the night Pop twisted so hard that he fell off the couch... there were long moments of silence...we didn't look at him...we didn't look at each other...there was neither snicker nor smile. We knew he was okay and we were all bursting inside, but we remained silent. He quickly scrambled back to his seat and we all rejoined the match. We never spoke of it that night, but retold the story hundreds of times at family gatherings!

While Russell was in high school and before he owned his first car, he bought a used Cushman motor scooter. He spent about as many hours repairing it as he did riding it. The first trial run was always around the block...about a quarter-mile. If all went well, he would attempt the hill on Christian Lane...about a three-mile round trip. He renamed that run Hard Luck Hill for reasons the reader can infer.

His first car was a 1948 Ford Sedan with four doors, whitewall tires, and a V8 engine. It was an elegant machine and while I am sure he had many good times in it without me, he did teach me to drive it and allowed me to wash and wax it almost every Sunday afternoon. I had to move and turn it around many times because he stressed that the paint should never be in the sun as it was being washed, dried, or waxed.

This was my introduction to the classic win-win situation. He had a beautifully clean car at all times and I got to drive alone every Sunday afternoon. Several years later when he entered the Army, he gave me his little Crosley station wagon as my car to drive to college: another win-win. I had a reliable car and he set himself up to buy something much better after his discharge.

College Years

Russell was noticed by football scouts during the two years he played on the semi-pro team in New Britain and was offered a full scholarship at Moorhead State College in Kentucky. By accepting the offer he became the first McCain to go to college. He left home early in August 1949 for the long bus ride to Kentucky.

An interesting cross-cultural episode took place on Russell's trip to Moorhead State. It was August, his first experience in the Old South, and he had developed an amazing tan working in construction all summer to get himself physically toughened and to earn spending money. As he boarded his connecting Greyhound bus in Washington, D.C., he greeted the driver and chose a seat across from him to have a better view. The driver studied his curly hair, broad shoulders and deep tan and decided Russell was a Yankee Negro. He figured he was either ignorant of the ways of the South or a smart aleck.

"Move to the back of the bus," the driver said.

"Why?" asked Russell. "I'd rather sit here so I can see where I'm going. It's my first trip down here."

"Don't get uppity with me, boy. This ain't New York City. In these parts your kind sits in the back of the bus. Now move!"

Suddenly Russell understood the problem: the driver thought he was black! "Oh, you think I'm a Negro. But I'm not, my name is Russ McCain," he said.

"Maybe you can pass in New York City, boy, but you can't pass down here. Now move to the back of the bus or get off!"

"I'll prove my point," he said.

Russell turned his back to the driver, mooned him briefly, then quietly took his seat at the front of the bus.

After Russell's departure for Moorhead State College I was more lonely than I would have expected. I was in about seventh grade and went to a four-room school built in 1774 and converted to a school in 1903. I was not very worldly. All I really knew was that he was far away and would not be back until Christmas. I was elated to hear he was coming home early and would arrive on October 18th, my birthday. His return was my best birthday gift that year, and he didn't go back to Kentucky!

In 1950, he enrolled at Teachers College of Connecticut as an Industrial Arts major, and he and David entered their freshman years together. He was a creative and outstanding student in the IA classes and, while he struggled some with the more academic parts of his curriculum, he was awarded his bachelor's degree in June 1955.

Russell was a true football star at TCC. He was a reliable and fast-thinking tackle who exploded from his stance faster than any other lineman. When the coaches called for ten-yard sprints, he beat every team member, including the fastest of the backs. On the hundred run, on the other hand, Russell routinely came in last. He was captain of the undefeated team and during his senior year was named as a runner-up in the New England competition for the Small College All American Football Team. He also threw the discus and the javelin for the TCC track team.

Russell visited me in the hospital during our freshman years: his at TCC and mine at Berlin High. I was having surgery to correct an injury from Little League. He was quite impressed with the Silly Putty that an earlier visitor had brought as a gift. We played with it for a while, stretching it, bouncing it, and using it to lift pictures from the newspaper. It was great fun. When he returned a few days later he sheepishly admitted that he had slipped a small sample into his pocket to show to friends. But it wasn't in his pocket when he reached for it. It had seeped through the fabric of his pocket and into both his slacks and his underwear. That one was a smiling lose-lose for both of us.

I was in high school while Russell attended TCC and in those years he coached me in many sports. He pitched to me on the neighborhood baseball field to help with my batting; he hit both grounders and high fly balls for me to chase down and catch. His "You're good at this!" still rings in my head and my heart. He taught me to hold and swing a tennis racquet and golf clubs, and to throw a discus, and he put me through the basics of football blocking. We spent many hours during my second high school summer playing tennis on the high school courts. He allowed me to play tennis lefty, but thought my righty swings were better in golf and baseball.

While attending TCC, Russell worked at the McAdoo Foundry. It was a part-time job during the school year and full time in the summer. His school-year assignments were often the type that could be done at any time of the day or night, so long as they were completed before the shop opened at six in the morning. This made it possible for him to play sports and be involved in other college activities. There were times when, after dropping off his prom date, he stopped at the foundry on his way home, changed from tuxedo to work clothes, and worked for a couple of hours, mixing the sand to be used for baking cores later that morning.

During his college years Russell would often bring home classmates who missed their own families and home-cooked meals. One of them was Dick Neville, a basketball and baseball player from Long Island. He probably visited more than any of the other guys and was as comfortable lying on the living room floor as any of the McCains, watching the games, telling stories, and enjoying each other's company.

Part III: Warm Recollections

Several years later when I was a TCC student, I was pleasantly surprised to learn I had been assigned to Mr. Neville for my Junior Student Teaching experience. He had just joined the college faculty as a teacher in the lab school, noticed my name on the list of candidates, and asked that I be assigned to him. Three years later, after he had become principal of an elementary school in Berlin, he invited me to teach sixth grade on his staff and I accepted. Dick became a close friend and advisor and was instrumental in my selection of Columbia University, New York City, as my graduate school.

One of our big family projects during Russell's TCC years was the construction of Pop's boat. Pop was a dedicated fisherman and spent most Sunday afternoons fishing from the edge of the various ponds in our area. Russell found a boat kit in the Sears Roebuck catalog. It was for an eight foot, square-front pram that would safely hold three fishermen. It came complete with oars and oarlocks and it was Pop's Father's Day gift from all of us. The plan was for us to assemble it in the cellar as a team. The kit came with what seemed to be a hundred pieces and a thousand screws. At one point we began to wonder if we could ever get it out of the cellar when we finished. Some very careful measuring followed, and it was deemed that removal would be possible but not easy.

Pop's beautiful green boat was launched in Turtle Pond. We had carried it the half-mile from home to the water, took our places on board and pushed off. It held all of us and did not leak! Later, Russell used old bicycle wheels and some pieces of pipe to build a push cart that made it easy for one person to wheel the boat to local fishing holes. We used a rooftop carrier to get to the more distant ones.

One summer evening Pop, Russell, and I drove to Cromwell, to the Connecticut River, so we could catch eels. Russell was in the stern running the motor, Pop was at the bow, and I was in the middle seat. My job was to fish, but also to be ready to unhook the eels if we caught any. The fisherman was to bring the eel in and lower it into my burlap sack. I'd grab the eel, sack and all, take out the hook and drop the eel into the sack. It turned out to be a busy night. The action was so fast that I never wet a line. As soon as one eel was off the hook, another was waiting. I'm not sure how many we caught that night, but Uncle George must have been really happy the next morning when Pop handed him a sack of eels. It was another win-win: Pop never ate fish, and Uncle George loved to cook and eat eels.

Russell, David, and I all graduated in 1955: they from college and me from high school. I don't remember their ceremony at all, but I do remember that I was fortunate enough to win a scholarship and three other awards at my graduation. When the ceremony was over Russell quietly said to our parents, "That deserves a present," and rushed home to get there before we could. When we arrived he congratulated me on my success at Berlin High and presented me with a nicely wrapped gift box. It held the electric shaver he had bought for himself just a few days earlier.

Russell also was instrumental in my admission to college. I had taken a strict college prep program in high school and TCC was the only college where I applied. I could live at home, and the costs matched our family resources. Some of my friends heard from their schools during the winter and others got letters in the early or late spring, but I heard nothing from my school. When it got to be August, I asked Russell for advice and he phoned Dr. Chatfield, one of his professors who had just been named Director of Admissions.

Dr. Chatfield found that my application was on file but not complete, since no transcript had arrived from Berlin High School. I raced to Berlin High, checked at main office, and found that my papers and transcript had been misfiled. They were mailed to the college that day, about August 8th. I received my acceptance letter on August 14th, registered for classes immediately, and started as a college freshman right after Labor Day 1955. I later learned that Russell and Dr. Chatfield worked together to speed my papers through the process to assure a September admission.

Teaching Career

Russell spent the last part of his senior college year teaching in Warwick, Rhode Island. The school needed an Industrial Arts teacher and agreed to offer him extra supervision so he could get credit for Senior Student Teaching as he finished out the school year on the Warwick payroll. Warwick was very different from Berlin. It was a tough school. It was Al Capone's home town and deserved its reputation. On his first day in class the department head introduced Russell by telling about his football experience and said something to the effect that Russell was in charge of the shop and he'd be happy to meet anyone who thought otherwise out behind the school to show them just how tough he was.

He was put to the test immediately when a student came up to ask a question and purposely dropped a large "C" clamp, barely missing Russell's toe. Russell handled the situation with such dispatch that, as a result, he cruised to the end of the school year with no more incidents.

Russell's next teaching job came as result of a phone call from Nick Solaway, a TCC classmate and football teammate. Canton High School was expanding its IA shops and program, and needed an IA teacher who could also coach football and track. Russell applied for the job and a long-term professional relationship grew from a football-based friendship. He and Nick were a successful teaching and coaching team for many years.

Early in Russell's teaching years at Canton, students began coming to school looking like the cast of the movie *Dirty Dancing*. Boys added metal taps to the heels their shoes and wore their shirts with the top three or four buttons open. The teachers were not pleased. Russell and Nick stood at the entrance to the IA department, checked every student, and told them to button up. If they had taps nailed to their shoes, the men removed them using shop tools. When students began to tear off buttons so they "...just can't button the shirt," the teachers took desk staplers from their shop jacket pockets and stapled the shirts close and tight at the neck. They told the students to come back at the end of the day with their staples still in place or suffer detention. Shoe taps and open shirt fronts quickly disappeared from the IA department.

Russell developed a foundry skills curriculum for Canton High and a small shop area was converted. Soon students were producing small castings. During his free time in the shop he crafted stunning life-sized bouquets of pewter flowers. At the request of Roger Carlson, a Canton teacher and track coach, Russell designed plans for a swinging cradle for newborns. (I don't know if his boys used one, but he gave a set of the plans to Tom and he built one that was used by Jodi, Scott and all five of his children).

One wintry morning when they were all living at home, the McCain teachers awoke to snow and a moment of history replayed itself. Tom was a student teacher in New Britain, David was an elementary teacher in Newington, and Russell was on the staff at

Canton High. Each was hoping his school would be closed for the day. After breakfast they sat in the living room, dressed only in undershorts and T-shirts listening, as they had years before, to the radio announcer reading the list of school closings. New Britain was called and Tom raced off to put on play clothes. Newington was next and David followed suit. After a long and anxious wait, Russell had to decide between putting on school clothes or being late for work. He reported for work and David and Tom played in the snow all day!

Army Years

The U.S. was involved in a "police action" in Korea. Russell had several friends who were in uniform, and at least one from Murray Heights lost his life in battle. Richard was already in the Army and Russell knew he was destined to join him. He gained some control over his destiny by volunteering to be drafted. This meant a three-year hitch and it gave him a choice around the timing. He reported for duty during the middle of the summer.

Part III: Warm Recollections

On the weekend before he was to report, Russell invited Tom on an overnight fishing and camping trip on the Connecticut River. They brought Pop's boat to Cromwell, loaded it with gear, locked the car, and set off. The plan was to fish all day, set up camp on an island in the middle of the river at Middle Haddam, and eat what was caught. The boating was fine, the fishing was good...the fire was excellent...the food was delicious...the island was private...the sleeping bags were warm...and the mosquitoes were under control. It was a wonderful good-bye party. They made one serious mistake though, and didn't know about it until the next day.

They were near a cliff at the side of the river when they caught the first fish big enough to keep. They had no stringer, so Russell reached up to the roots hanging from the cliff, cut off two six-inch pieces and tied them to the ends of a length of fishing line. It was a fine stringer for holding dinner. Other fish were added and all were kept in the water to stay fresh. The roots were poison ivy, to which Russell was highly allergic. He reported to basic training with a raging, blistery rash.

He arrived home in uniform on a Friday evening a week or so after he had left, and he had a wonderful story to tell. His company had been assigned to a brand new barracks for their basic training. One morning they were standing in formation, and the Master Sergeant asked if any of them was an experienced cabinet maker. Russell raised hand and was sent to the company commander, who asked if he could immediately get his tools to the base and build some bulletin boards for the barracks. Russell said a quick, "Yes sir!" to each question and was given a three-day pass.

Fortunately Pop had gotten a set of handyman tools the prior Christmas. They included the basic hand tools for homeowners, packaged in a gray metal, suitcase-style case, roughly two feet by three feet and six inches deep. They became Russell's official cabinet-maker tools and, best of all, they were designed for travel. Russell returned to basic training and spent much of the next six weeks designing and building furnishings requested by the captain. He attended only the weapons training and a few other required classes. As part of the arrangement, he came home one weekend to pick up "another important tool" and a third time to return all tools to his "cabinet-maker shop," which looked a lot like Pop's work bench in the cellar.

It was during the first visit that Russell described how difficult it was for him in basic training. He was an experienced teacher and five or six years older than most of the recruits and many of their trainers. "Dopey kids like the worst I've ever had in my class are now screaming at me and telling me what to do. It's hard for me to stay in control," he told his college student brother Tom. "Do yourself a favor and join the Army Reserve. You'll earn some much easier basic training. And do it right away." Tom enlisted at the Army Reserve Center within days.

After finishing basic training and enjoying a short leave at home, Russell's company was sent by plane to Korea, with a short stopover in Japan. As the troops were standing in line in Japan, about to board the Korea flight, a loud voice called out, "McCain!" Russell responded and was pulled from the group. Apparently some phone calls had been made about him. He played on the base football team for at least two seasons. When he was not playing football, he worked a desk job in Army Intelligence.

Later, as Russell was preparing to leave Japan, he told his coach that David, an excellent football player, swimming coach and lifeguard, was currently on his way to Korea on the same flight schedule Russell had taken months earlier. The coach also had David pulled from the line at the airport and he spent his active duty years in Japan playing football. During his off season he was a swim coach and lifeguard at the Base Officers Club pool.

Except for football season, Russell had most weekends free. He bought a new motor scooter when his first season was over and used it often to tour Japan. On the day of the purchase, a friend gave him a ride to the dealership, which was a good distance from the base. During the trip home he feared he had bought a lemon and sad memories of Hard Luck Hill raced into his mind.

It had turned cold and started to snow. Worse, it seemed that the scooter had more and more trouble climbing hills as they got further away from the dealership. No matter how hard he pulled up on the accelerator, the motor just chugged up the hills, seemingly slower each time. He began to wonder if he would make it to the base. He was cold and tired, and he was getting more disappointed with each half-mile and every hill.

Then he realized his snow-cold fingers were so stiff that although it felt like he was giving the motor plenty of gas, he didn't have enough strength in his fingers to pull up on the gas lever. He parked at the side of the road, opened his jacket and slid his hand into an armpit for a several minutes. When he started the engine again it sprang life and climbed eagerly up the hills. He had to stop several more times to thaw his hands, but he made it back safely.

In one letter to the family he pointed out, with some wonder, the oneness of the world. He was on the other side of the world, and yet the thread size and pitch of bolts and nuts were universal. He could buy in a Japanese hardware store parts he needed to fix a scooter built in the USA.

He bought a Nash Metropolitan Roadster when he was discharged. It was a green-and-cream- colored beauty and his first new car.

Back to Canton and More

Pop was not very socially active in the 1950s but he never missed bowling on Wednesday nights. McAdoo Foundry sponsored a team in the New Britain Industrial League and one of Pop's fondest dreams was to head a team of himself and his boys. We saw a totally different version of Pop when we were together at the alleys. He talked and joked with nearly everyone and became quite competitive when it was his turn to bowl.

Bowling night was a good time for us to get together too. We could talk family business;

chat about work, wives, kids and girlfriends; and occasionally ask Richard to swap cars with us and fix a problem. We took turns pumping gas at his Shell station on Saturday mornings so he could work on cars without being interrupted. Then we would swap cars back again.

In August 1959 Tom and Sandra were married. Russell was best man and, since David was away at Army Reserve camp, Tom's high school pal Pete Schoech and Richard were the ushers.

Russell and Sarah were married the following year.

In the early 1960s Russell was elected president of the Canton Teachers Association and was invited to attend a state-wide meeting run by the CEA. It was an orientation for new presidents of local associations. David was also at the meeting as president of Newington Education Association, as was Tom, who had been elected by the Berlin Education Association. It was the first time ever for the CEA that three brothers were local presidents at the same time.

Soon after that year Russell was invited by the CEA to be a part-time field representative while he continued to teach and coach in Canton. It was also about that time that Tom accepted a school principalship in New Jersey. Sandra and Tom moved in August 1964.

A couple of years after Tom and Sandra were in New Jersey, Russell and Sarah went to visit them so Russell and Tom could talk about a career opportunity. The CEA had offered Russell a full-time field service position and he asked Tom to review with him potential possibilities and pitfalls. Russell took the position and remained with the CEA for many years until he retired.

He became one of the strongest and most successful negotiators on the CEA staff. At times he was chosen to oppose private professional negotiators, often lawyers, some districts hired to represent them in the talks. Russell's reputation within that group was as a strong strategist, a hard bargainer, and an honest competitor.

In 1966 Jodi Beth became a member of the family, having come to live with Sandra and

Tom when she was five days old. Russell and other family members drove to New Jersey for her baptism, at which he became Jodi's godfather.

Several years later Tom became a superintendent of schools in New Jersey. When he attended his first superintendents' meeting he was approached by Jim Moran, Executive Secretary of the New Jersey Association of School Administrators, who asked if he knew Russ McCain. When Tom said they were brothers, Moran replied, "I've negotiated for a few Connecticut school districts and met up with Russ several times. He is the toughest and straightest negotiator I ever worked against. If you're anything like him, you'll be an asset to our association. Welcome."

At one time the negotiations in Tom's district had hit a particularly rough patch, with picketers and demonstrators carrying anti-administration slogans shouting at them. He phoned Russell for advice. "Don't take it personally," he said. "It's not you they're shouting about, it's the superintendent. They would have been coached to say those things, whoever was in your job."

As Russell's career with the CEA was coming to a close, he and Tom had another serious discussion. The CEA offered him a choice between a life-long pension based on his earnings there, or a lump sum separation package. Each had advantages and disadvantages. It was after these thorough discussions that he made his decision.

Several years later, after they had both retired from education, Tom phoned Russell in Florida to say he was scheduled to present a day-long seminar at a hotel in Tampa. He invited Russell to share a dinner there and, if he chose, to attend the seminar as well. "I told Sarah I was going," he said after thinking about it for a day or two, "and said if she and Mary wanted to come with me, they could." All three came, sat in on part of the seminar, and shared a meal in Tampa.

Part IV. Unexpected Treasure

Chapter 21: Letters

Sometimes unexpected things happen in a good way. I'm not talking about the sudden positive "ah-hahs" or "oh-my-goshes" of the world but, instead, the slow and steady positive surprises that result from unintended but habitual behavior, such as emptying your pockets every day after school or work and saving all of your coins in a jar over a long period of years and finding you have accumulated enough money to buy a nice gift. Or, in a priceless and immeasurable way, such as the wealth of a treasure trove of letters from my Dad, saved over a 30-plus year period.

My Dad was a great letter writer. Not in a fanciful, linguistic way but, rather, in a constantly reminding you he was there for you way, what home was like way, guiding you through historical family events such as births, promotions, weddings, sicknesses and retirements way, and just, well, just reminding you that he loved you way.

I never set out to save his letters, keep them for prosperity or collectability's sake, or certainly with the intent to ever share them. It's just that, well, I could never bear to throw any of them away. He didn't have any more or less spare time than the rest of us, and yet he always took the time to find the right thing to say at the right time, or, to simply remind me that whatever my station in life, he was always around the figurative corner waiting and there for me. For that I am and always will be both grateful and simply further amazed at his greatness as a human being.

While I know I can't possibly share all of his letters or the masses of cards he used to send on all of the silly, ancillary, card-sending occasions we have in the States, I am happy, and more importantly proud, to share with you the letters I do have.

4 December 1980

Dave,

Enclosed is the material I received from Art.

Also, I drafted a sample letter and resume. You may use them, edit them, combine them or disregard. Hopefully they'll all be of help.

Went to see Mama last night. She is nowhere near as uncomfortable or painful as she was on Monday but is quite spaced at times because of the medication, but, still cheerful and most often alert, interested and beautiful.

Keep you posted, looking forward to seeing and hearing from you.

Love, Dad

I Love You Dad

29 October 1982

Dear Dave,

Enclosed is the full packet of materials received from the LSAT.

Amidst the disappointment I see some bright spots, the first of which is that this was a new testing form, therefore lacking the validation of time and standardized norms.

Second, you did extremely well on the logic section, which seems to me is more innate and difficult to acquire and learn than reading comprehension, and, is certainly less affected or influenced by the high anxiety and emotions created from wanting to do so well on one short test.

Third, and not reflected at all in the test score, are all of the other traits and characteristics that are infinitely more contributing to a prognosis of success by whomever is involved in such a judgment. Your purpose, commitment, character and ability to relate with people is so respected and exceptional that you will not be lacking in assistance and help to go where you want to go.

Part IV. Unexpected Treasure

I also believe, that if at all possible, it would be much to your advantage to arrange for a personal interview along with your application, in those schools that interest you the most.

Whatever, these are some thoughts I pass along for your consideration.

I do know that you know the difference between disappointment and disaster and that this particular score is not a disaster.

Also, you know that you have my perpetual confidence and love.

Love,

Dad

PS Looking forward to seeing you for the weekend.

28 February 1989

Dear Dave,

Can you believe it, not even used to writing 1989 yet and February has gone by.

Ten more days and I'll be putting on sun-tan lotion.

Enclosed is the article on Tellier I spoke about last night.

See you soon!

Hi to Margarita and Johnny!

Love, Dad

4 April 1989

Dear Dave,

Boy does time fly, with daylight savings now in effect winter is definitely gone, and still day light when you get home from work.

I've enclosed an article which was in last night's paper regarding the "Leather Man." Remember I mentioned him in the car on the day we visited the Keys. A fascinating story but also of interest is that the writer is from St. Paul Catholic High School (do you remember him?). I have met him; he is a friend of Ron.

Part IV. Unexpected Treasure

The other bit of info regards Washington DC tours, and costs, for your drive up this summer.

Well, the kitchen cabinets are in, minus the stove which has been back-ordered, but we are still not functioning. The state of wiring in the house required some heavy electrical work, starting from replacing the main fuse box, and then rewiring all outlets and switches in the kitchen. So, we have the coffee maker set up on a TV tray and the refrigerator running off an extension cord from the front room. Needless to say, it's been an eating out week (except over the weekend, we used the grill). However, the electrical work is supposed to be completed tonight. That just leaves the floor (which someone else will install), the ceiling and the walls to take care of.

The cellar currently looks like a disaster area. All the old cabinets are down there, plus the electrician's mess, but, when I finish installing the old cabinets it will look and be nice. Coincidentally, the old kitchen counter fits perfectly in the cabinet work bench area so that will be great with all the storage cabinets underneath it.

Stopped up at the club to see Gary about the clubs. When the practice range opens up (next week) I'll try several kinds, get a lesson, etc., tough life right? Hope you've had a chance to try out the executives; I'm interested to see how you like them.

Also, fishing season opens April 15, so you can see it's really getting into my busy season which is good because it will help time fly till summer when I'll be seeing you all up here.

Again, we had a great time on our visit. Mom is still talking about the "estate" you brought us to.

Say hello and give my love to Margarita and Johnny.

See you,

Love, Dad

Part IV. Unexpected Treasure

10 May 1989

Dear Dave,

To keep you abreast of the St. Paul High School situation, it looks like Bishop Whealon has successfully passed the accountability of keeping the school open to the parents. So, that's news—bad news.

In another area, we have bought a car to replace the '83 Skyhawk, a new four door Honda Civic–gold.

Your mother grew to enjoy auto shopping and practically got addicted but I'm sure she'll tell you blow by blow of "he said...we said."

Hey, realize we're down to counting weeks again?

Love, Dad

20 October 1989

Dear Dave,

Here's the letter from the state Insurance Dept.

Also, for no particular reason, a set of definitions I found in my files while cleaning up. Hope you can use them.

Really hope that you did well at the Dr.'s today.

Love to Margarita and Johnny.

Love, Dad

PS—rushing because the mailman is here!

1 November 1989

Dear Dave,

Here's your letter from Brown.

Well, we survived Halloween in great shape; all eleven kids showed up and we knew them all. Not like the old days with the roving bands of "older" kids with pillowcases full of collected treats.

I'm sure the light drizzle also kept many from travelling too far.

The only expected ones that didn't show were Ed and his two little ones (he now also

Part IV. Unexpected Treasure

has custody of the girl). But, we don't see him anywhere near as much since his parents moved back to Bristol.

Also, no soap, smashed pumpkins, or trashed mailboxes, really quiet!

I think we've turned into a retirement neighborhood.

Hope your Halloween was also fun and pleasant.

Looking forward to seeing you all,

Love, Dad

28 November, 1989

Dear Dave,

I'm forwarding a couple of (too close) pictures of my new car—taken November 24, 1989, the day after Thanksgiving. We had a very wonderful time, but you and yours were missed and send their regards.

Additionally, I've tossed in two pictures of the deck—one of 24 November and the other just a few months earlier.

Also on this reel were the pictures of the "new" kitchen I took to send you in July—sorry!

Finally, a clipping from the Hartford Courant to let you know that last year's bear sighting wasn't that novel.

Just think, in only a few weeks we'll be seeing all of you. Really looking forward to it.

Love, Dad

December 1989

Dear Dave,

Enclosed is a copy of a letter I received from Canada.

Please add whatever appropriate info you can and return it to me so I can get it back to Rita.

Also, I'll ask her for a copy of the completed project.

Hope you're feeling totally ok. For cheer I've enclosed more shots from my new camera—great huh?

Part IV. Unexpected Treasure

See you very soon!

Love, Dad

January 1990

Dear Dave, Margarita, Johnny,

Here is a sample of the new camera. As you can see, it's great under all sorts of conditions.

Even more, it was a wonderful time.

Enjoy,

See you in a matter of weeks,

Love, Dad

19 January 1990

Dear Dave,

Talk about quality time, what a great visit and Christmas we had. Hope your birthday is also wonderful. We are really looking forward to March. See you then.

Love, Mom and Dad

PS Was hoping to enclose some pictures but they're not in yet

20 March 1990

Dear Dave and Margarita,

Here's a trip sheet and info for a Bristol, CT —Nova Scotia journey plus other material. Hope it provides much help for another great trip.

Again, thanks for a wonderful time in March.

Looking forward to seeing you this summer.

Love, Dad

2 May 1990

Dear Dave,

Enclosed are the newspaper article and the "Outstanding Young Men" material.

Part IV. Unexpected Treasure

I've also thrown in a copy of my birth certificate. I think I'd better get it laminated and order a certified copy from Nashua before it falls apart totally.

I did get things squared away at Social Security, so that's a relief.

Hope things are going well. Say hello to all.

Love, Dad

Dear Dave,

Here are the newspaper articles about Jeff's wedding. What a lovely thing to happen.

The Hotel is rather new and is nice. It enjoys a very good restaurant and reputation (or did).

Your Mother and I had a very nice dinner there last Valentine's Day.

In preparation for next Tuesday's (June 12) Member/Guest at Wethersfield with Bob and Art, I stopped at Chippanee this AM on the way to work and made an appointment with Gary for a lesson (I hope one will get me started right). But I figure if I don't start acting like a "ringer" pretty soon they won't be asking me back very often. I'll let you know how it goes.

In the interim, say "Hi" to all,

Love, Dad

20 September 1990

Dear Dave,

Congratulations on your recognition and raise at work.

We're very pleased, proud and happy for you. It does make the sun shine a little longer each day doesn't it! I'm glad things are going so well.

I talked to Uncle Tom last night. Scott is down in your area somewhere going to naval Flight School. I don't know exactly where, or what his schedule demands but you may or may not get a call sometime in the future. How's that for being "newsy." Also, I'm enclosing an article on your former track *coach. He's doing very well in Canton too, as you can see. When we talk, he often asks about you so he has a general idea of what you've been up to.*

Again, congratulations.

Love, Dad

18 October 1990

Dear Dave,

Here's the fraternity material you asked to have forwarded.

Hope your Chicago trip was both worthwhile and enjoyed.

Believe it or not, still getting to the Boys Club every weekday AM between 6:00 and 6:30. I am now up to 24 laps (one lap is 60 feet) in a half hour, not bad. The first week I really struggled to do 14 laps but I'm learning to breathe; it helps.

Also have enclosed a new card because it includes our new fax number which we have just acquired.

Love and regards to all, Dad

I Love You Dad

26 April, 1991

Dear Dave,

We got your very nice Anniversary card along with your pictures. Thanks very much.

Here's another try at getting these pictures to you.

I'm always impressed that it seems like perpetual vacation time in every picture from Florida.

Darn, just had the bathroom fixed and done all over and found that it still leaks when showering. In a way I'm glad because I really felt stupid in not being able to find the leak, but it has evidently evaded the plumber too, and now it's his problem.

Last night after work, your Mother and I went and bought a new liner for the pool (sale at NAMCO's) so I guess that will be one of the big projects in an upcoming weekend.

The past few days have been classic, fresh and spring-like, every tree and bush is practically exploding popcorn-like with greenery. A very beautiful and refreshing time of the year after a long winter. So for this weekend at last, forget the liner. Chippanee beware!

Bye for now,

Love, Dad

May 1990

Dear Dave,

As promised, here are some copies of the pictures taken at Mom's retirement party. There were a number of other full tables of people from her bank connections and unknown to me so I didn't forward them. All together there were 45—50 people there. Some pictures, yet to be developed are not included.

You know it was a total surprise because she wore the same outfit to the party that she wore to work that day! Enjoy.

Looking forward to seeing you all this summer.

Love, Dad

PS Doesn't the dress fit and look great?

7 June 1991

Dear Dave,

Thought you, Margarita and Johnny would enjoy last night's front page of the Bristol Press.

In other news, your Mother is very much enjoying retired life. She hasn't overslept one morning yet and is busy being busy.

The bathroom is almost completed. We've ended up having a new tub and shower unit, new floor and all new tile, as well as the sink, toilet and vanity being replaced. Ten years ago we could have added a garage and breezeway for the same price.

Hope your house and schedules are still moving along well. Can't wait to see it! It all sounds great and I don't know how it seems to you but from here it seems that you've gotten a lot accomplished already.

Boy has my golf game fallen off. I was planning to play this weekend in the member/member, but for some reason I've become totally inconsistent and not playing to my handicap at all, probably just some little thing. I should break down and take a lesson from Gary.

Your Mother is taking lessons in Southington, along with Aunt Mary, Karen, and Scrubs. Their teacher is the baseball coach you used to have that wanted you to forgo all other sports and just concentrate on baseball. He keeps announcing to the whole class as to what a great pitcher you were and the talent, and the attitude and how far you could have gone, etc., etc.

Your Mother is tuning up for the Bristol Girls Club tournament to be played this coming week. Mary, Karen, and Scrubs just want to learn how to play and they all are having fun at the lessons.

Work has been quite busy of late, mostly niggling little things that are brought to the surface because the school year is coming to a close. In a couple of weeks it should all pass and we'll be back to normal.

I'm going to sign off now so this can catch the mailman.

Love and regards to all, Dad

18 June 1991

Dear Dave, Margarita, Johnny and Sparky,

Thanks so much for the card, golf balls and shirt. I haven't hit the balls yet but I did wear the shirt to the "New England Clam Bake and Lobster Night" at Pequabuck Golf Club last Saturday night. The shirt was a perfect fit, and looked good on me. The clam bake was also fun in that George and Mary, all of their kids and spouses, as well as Tim and Debi, were there too. We had a good time and there was even live music, but in no way could it be compared to the kind of 'lobster" evening we had at Chippanee last summer at the Member/Guest weekend.

With regard to Chippanee, I've enclosed some more "bear" news to follow up the last clipping I sent. As you know, a week ago last Sunday there was a bear sighting reported at 116 Delmar Drive. Your mother, Mary, George, and I went looking for it (by car) but never did see anything except a growing number of eyewitnesses.

Hope things are still going along well at your place without too many unforeseen snags, and that your "to do" list is shrinking on schedule.

Again, thanks. Just think, we'll be seeing you in about seven weeks and by then, your house should also be in pretty good shape.

Looking forward to it!

Love, Dad

4 October 1991

Dear Dave,

Thought you might enjoy this article by Dave L. I can see why he's following journalism as a career.

Fall is definitely here; not only has the Mum Parade been marched, but the leaves are all beginning to turn. It's time to pack up and cover the pool until next spring. Darn, I really got used to using it a lot this past summer, but it's easier to get it going next year if I cover it before it fills with leaves.

Still pondering your find. Could this lift be the type used to hoist cargo into an airplane? I forgot to ask what sort of base it has.

We just had a strange problem resolved here. Lights in the house have been flickering for some time and early this week they would actually go out and then come back on. We had the electrician check all internal wiring and the new service panel, all were okay. The problem was in the electric meter outside. Seems that when they built the house 30 plus years ago they mixed copper and aluminum wires. The two reacted chemically and corroded. So, they just finished fixing it today.

Regards to all.

Love, Dad

22 November 1991

Dear Dave and Margarita,

The ring sounds great, can't tell you how much I appreciate your help. I've enclosed a check.

Part IV. Unexpected Treasure

Even more, it's wonderful that you can make it up for Christmas. I'm really looking forward to it, along with everyone else. Hope the weather cooperates so that we have a picture postcard setting.

Also, congratulations to Johnny, WAY TO GO! I'm enclosing a decal from a tip-top contender and definite threat to the University of Miami should they get out of their league.

He may want to display it in a prominent place.

Meanwhile, thanks again,

Love, Dad

16 April 1993

Dear Dave and Margarita,

Here are some pictures you might enjoy, the first few show how March began, the second few how April began.

Today I'm going back to Hopkinton to pick up your Mom. She's been there for three days. I brought her on Wednesday the day Debi's parents left. I suspect by now Tim, Debi and Christopher can use a little time alone by themselves. Debi is feeling much better, taking walks and can now drive. Christopher is sleeping four to five hours at a time during the night and is behaving very well. Tim has the weekend off.

Things are going well for me also, obviously back to work with no problems. I have a preliminary meeting next Thursday with Tom M., CEA executive, to explore retirement. I'll keep you posted.

Just got interrupted by a phone call from Cheryl McCain telling me that Uncle David is in the hospital awaiting an operation on his heel. Seems like yesterday he was at the Cape opening up the cottage and the stairs on the back deck gave way, causing a bad fall. He then drove himself to the Hyannis Hospital where they put him in a cast and told him he needed reconstructive surgery on his heel. He opted to have Cheryl come and pick him up and bring him home to his own doctor. So, he is in the New Britain General Hospital, 100 Grand Street, New Britain, CT

Part IV. Unexpected Treasure

06050. I just called him and he is a little groggy and waiting for surgery.

I'll keep you posted.

In the meantime,

Love to all,

Dad

20 January 1993

Dear Dave,

Hope you had a wonderful 32nd birthday. Doesn't time go by too fast? Seems like I was just watching you in the playpen, or with the party hat stuck under your chin.

The movies and photos bring back a flood of memories over all the years, and I want you to know that you've made me happy for you and proud of you for all of them. See you.

Love, Dad

21 November 1994

Dear Dave and All,

Just got some pictures back and thought you might enjoy seeing what it was like here while your Mom was in Florida a few weeks ago. She also missed it! As you can see, in addition to the color, the weather was also beautiful. Actually, these pictures were taken about a week after the foliage peak, but still quite stunning.

Yesterday, Mom, I, Tony, and Lucy went to see the N.E. Patriots upset the Chargers. It was also a great day weather-wise and we tailgated before and after the game with two other families and a bunch of kids from Bristol. It reminded me so much of some of the good old days in the past.

Last Wednesday, we went to see Courtney Sarah, and at a few hours old she seemed to be quite cute, and fortunately she and Debi did very well. Your mother and Tim did too! We took Christopher home with us for a couple of days, a real treat and delight for us. We brought him back on Friday when Debi returned home. We're going back to

Part IV. Unexpected Treasure

Hopkinton this Wednesday and staying over for Thanksgiving and, however longer if we can be of help.

The next set of pictures you see will probably be of snow drifts, but I expect to be delivering those personally.

I hope all is well with all of you and that you have a wonderful Thanksgiving. Isn't there so much to be thankful and celebrate for!

Love, Dad

PS I'm feeling fine too!

14 October 1997

Dear Dave,

Hope you have all had a very pleasant and enjoyable respite at Hilton Head. I've enclosed the article about Dave L.; hope you enjoy it and the photos.

I'm happy to be finally able to get around and feel a little independent, now that I can get my own shoes on, walk around and drive. Stairs and uneven ground are still a little challenge but I can handle them. Even played two sets of nine holes of golf so far, so things are really looking up!

Interestingly, as I get more mobile and active the swelling in the leg decreases, enough so that tomorrow I'm having the leg brace reshaped to fit more snugly, which means that now I'll have to help your Mom rake the leaves in the front yard. They're brilliantly colored, especially the maples, but really plentiful. If she hadn't raked up and bagged so many, they would probably be knee-deep under the maples and they aren't even half shed yet! It's been an exceptionally beautiful year for foliage so far, plus we've been enjoying a most pleasant "Indian Summer" for the past two weeks, which is about to break into the cool fall days very soon.

Looking forward to the Thanksgiving celebration.

See you soon,

Love, Dad

Part IV. Unexpected Treasure

25 June 1999

Dear Dave and Margarita,

Again, thanks for the Father's Day wine gift, very nice, and what class, not only very well packaged and presented, as I said, but, today I received this enclosed letter and wine description which also included this card and stamped envelope for my use.

Again, thanks for a very nice and thoughtful gift.

Love, Dad

30 December 2003

Dear Daniel,

You recently asked me to share some of my memories of the "Depression Years" of the 1930s and of World War II.

My parents were both from New Hampshire and I was born Nashua, NH, in 1931. I already had an older brother, Richard, who was three and in 1933 another brother David, was born. In 1934 we moved to

Connecticut because the foundry where my father was employed was bought and moved to New Britain, CT. We were fortunate in that he was never unemployed.

Our house was in a rural setting in the outskirts of the city of New Britain, CT. At one time it was a working farm and still had a big hay loft, chicken coop, shed, and privies (two outdoor toilets). However, it is now modernized with electricity, running water, indoor flush toilets and an indoor kitchen stove that burned wood, which was later upgraded to burn kerosene. Some of the local farmers stored extra hay in our barn but we only used it for a garage. The chicken coop was used. We always had a couple of dozen layers (hens that lay eggs) and a rooster or two. The shed was used for storing chicken feed, garden tools, etc.

In 1937 my youngest brother, Thomas, was born. There weren't many other kids in the neighborhood because the houses were so far apart. Tommy was way younger than the rest of us so we three older boys did a lot together, both in playing and in chores. Some chores were assigned and some were understood. For example, it was understood that you scraped the mud off your shoes, cleaned up your own spilled milk, picked up your own mess, etc. After meals we rotated the chores of cleaning off the table, washing the dishes, and drying and putting away the dishes. By the time I was five, one of my main chores was the chickens. I had to scrape the roost and feed and water the chickens every day. Occasionally I had to gather the eggs, but my Mom usually did that. From the spring to late summer we spent a lot of time doing chores in the garden. We had quite a big one and grew almost everything you find in a grocery store today. We didn't have freezers then, so my mother canned hundreds of jars of vegetables, pickles, jellies, jams, fruits, juices, sauces, etc. It was a lot of hard work for all of us that culminated in a lot of satisfaction and accomplishment.

Saturday night was bath night for us boys. Other nights of the week we washed up with a wash bowl of warm water, a bar of soap and a wash cloth, but on Saturdays, after our sponge bath, we actually got into the tub (we had no shower). The reason for this was that originally all the water had to be heated by kettle on the kitchen stove. Originally we all got in together but that didn't last too long and we had to wait our turn. Richard, Russell, and then David. Between each one, another kettle of hot water was added to what was already there. You can see why it all had to be preceded by a sponge bath. In the summer, should there be a warm day and heavy shower we would go out on the lawn in our bathing suits with a bar of soap and run around, wrestle and play.

On Saturday nights and Sunday nights we would all sit in our favorite chairs and listen to the radio, which had very good reception because the antenna stretched from the roof of the house to the barn. I remember Jack Benny, The Shadow, Inner Sanctum, *and* others.

Also, my Dad put in some horseshoe pits next to the barn. In the evening the men used to come and pitch shoes. They enjoyed it so much they eventually put up a light so they could continue after dark.

Part IV. Unexpected Treasure

A big event twice a year for us kids was when they mowed the hay. On one side of our house we had a large garden and some fruit trees, on the other side was a very large hay field, corn field, and clover field. Anyway, we couldn't wait until almost the whole field was mowed, leaving only one small parcel to be cut. When the mower started into that section all types of varmints and critters came running out. You'd be amazed at the kinds of birds, rodents, reptiles, and creatures that lived there.

It was probably because of living in the semi-rural setting, with the good neighbors and my hard-working and wonderful parents, that I cannot remember ever feeling deprived, poor or unfortunate during the depression years. I do recall however, being aware of all the candy one could get for just a couple of pennies at the local store. That eventually became the meaning of "being rich" to me: having enough cash to buy enough candy so that I would always have some in my pocket for sharing or eating later. I've since learned that this isn't the best definition of "rich," but I do admit that in the subsequent years and even until now I always carry some gum or mints in my pocket.

Later into the 1930s the news on the radio spoke more and more about a war in Europe. The bad guys were the Nazis in Germany and they were over-running the smaller countries. England, France, and Russia were the good guys and we were on their side. We were "Allies." In the Far East, Japan was the bad guy and they were invading China, our friend and ally. It was the beginning of World War II and we started getting ready.

Sunday, December 7, 1941: the news on the radio told us about Japan bombing Pearl Harbor. We wondered what would happen. My Dad was too old to be drafted into the military and my brothers and I were too young. I had four cousins who lived in New Hampshire that enlisted in the service: Olin, Paul, Raymond, and Edwin McAdoo. They went into the Army, Navy, Marines, and Navy respectively. They also had four younger sisters: Marion, Andrea, Alena, and Colleen. They were all just about the ages of me and my brothers. So, my Uncle George and Aunt Pauline had four blue stars hanging in their windows. That meant that the family had four sons in the service. Later, one star was changed to gold, meaning one son got killed on Iwo Jima, an island in the Pacific Ocean.

All sorts of stuff was collected for recycling into the war effort: scrap metal, tin cans, aluminum pots, old rubber tires, rags, newspapers, milkweed pods for life preservers, etc. Even people who never had a garden before started "victory gardens" because some things became scarce and hard to get. Certain foods like sugar, meat, coffee, and butter were rationed and the government issued ration books for each person to regulate how much each family could use during a certain period of time. I remember needing to bring my ration book for those times that I went to Boy Scout camp in summer. Gasoline was also rationed by the gallon and you couldn't buy it without a ration stamp.

Along the coasts and in major cities we exercised what was called "blackout." That is, at night no lights could be showing. No street lights on, no store signs, and all homes had to have their windows covered so no light would shine through. This was done so that enemy submarines, lurking off our shores, could not silhouette an American ship or freighter against the shore light and torpedo it. They were quite skilled and successful at this.

Later, in the Boy Scouts, I studied to be an "airplane spotter." We had to learn all the names and types of the military aircraft of both the Allies and the Axis.

I used to write to my cousins and other friends in the service. We were encouraged to do so because it was good for morale, and we thought it was patriotic to let them know how much we cared. It was usually done on "V" mail, which was a very thin, tough, single sheet of paper with dotted lines on one side. You wrote your letter on one side, then turned it over and folded on the dotted lines. That turned it into its own envelope that you addressed and mailed. It saved a lot of space for shipping.

As I entered my high school years the war came to an end, first in Europe and then the Far East. The fighting was over at last, but sadly, it did not live up to what we wanted so much to believe at the time. We really thought that World War II and the horrific things that it begot would be the "war to end all wars." Sadly that's not so. I hope you guys do better.

Danny, I hope this is of some help with your projects. Looking forward to seeing you in a few weeks.

Love, Grandpa Russell

9 May 2007

Dear Dave,

I've found the pictures relating to the story I told regarding Uncle Arthur's farm in Canada.

Recap: Arthur Ord was my father's uncle. At the time of these pictures he was in his late 70s. His family, originally from Scotland, homesteaded the farm under a land grant in Cookshire, Canada, near Sherbrooke, Canada.

I Love You Dad

In 1958 I was teaching school in Canton, CT, with Nick, a very close friend and good fishing buddy. I often told him about how good the fishing was in the brook that ran through Uncle Arthur's farm and fed into the farm pond.

I told him I would go out before breakfast each morning, fish only in the brook, and photograph my catch. On the farm, breakfast was served after the morning chores were done. As I recall, the brook was small enough so that in many places you could jump across it, but it was quite deep. In less than two hours I had a full creel.

I posed the fish several ways on a big flat rock and took close up shots to make them appear even bigger.

My Dad attested to Nick that the time period and fish count were true. Needless to say, Nick was flabbergasted. Even to this day, I secretly smile when I think of the fish story he bought.

Love, Dad

Part IV. Unexpected Treasure

PS Would you believe Uncle Arthur even had me put maple sugar syrup on the fried trout? (Mmm—not bad.)

PSS Note the carafe of maple syrup on the breakfast table.

Final letter:

22 April, 2013

Dear Dad,

I Love you. I miss you, and look forward, should God deem me worthy, of seeing, being, and walking with you in heaven.

Love,

David

I Love You Dad

It's interesting that two simple syllables can be packed with so much emotion. I felt a surge of emotion as I read "The Drive" and immediately was back to my final phone conversation with your Dad. He shared many of the details with me, and said often that "David really came through like a champ." Carry that in your heart, my friend: your final act of love and kindness to your Dad was recognized, appreciated, and lauded by him, even in his final hours!

—Thomas McCain

Wow. Thank you. What a wonderful piece. I remember when Grandpa died, Dad was so worried whether he was able to show Grandpa that he was anywhere near as good a father/son that Grandpa had been. You were lucky enough to have that moment, prolonged for three days, where you left no doubt. I am sure Dad was incredibly proud of this final gift. A well done and poignant story.

—Tim McCain

I Love You Dad

David McCain is a husband, dad, son, brother, nephew, and uncle living in Coral Gables, Florida. He holds an undergraduate degree in Political Science from Brown University and a JD from the University of Miami School of Law.

I Love You Dad